W9-CGW-548

THE PAPILLON

Tammy Gagne

The Papillon

Project Team
Editor: Mary E. Grangeia
Copy Editor: Joann Woy
Indexer: Elizabeth Walker
Designer: Angela Stanford
Series Design: Stephanie Krautheim and Mada Design
Series Originator: Dominique De Vito

T.F.H. Publications
President/CEO: Glen S. Axelrod
Executive Vice President: Mark E. Johnson
Publisher: Christopher T. Reggio
Production Manager: Kathy Bontz

T.F.H. Publications, Inc.
One TFH Plaza
Third and Union Avenues
Neptune City, NJ 07753

Copyright © 2010 by T.F.H. Publications, Inc.

All rights reserved. No part of this publication may be reproduced, stored, or transmitted in any form, or by any means electronic, mechanical or otherwise, without written permission from T.F.H. Publications, except where permitted by law. Requests for permission or further information should be directed to the above address.

Printed and bound in China
06 07 08 09 10 1 3 5 7 9 8 6 4 2
Library of Congress Cataloging-in-Publication Data
Gagne, Tammy.
  The Papillon / Tammy Gagne.
     p. cm.
  Includes index.
  ISBN 978-0-7938-3689-5 (alk. paper)
  1. Papillon dog. I. Title.
  SF429.P2G34 2010
  636.76--dc22
                    2009026112

This book has been published with the intent to provide accurate and authoritative information in regard to the subject matter within. While every reasonable precaution has been taken in preparation of this book, the author and publisher expressly disclaim responsibility for any errors, omissions, or adverse effects arising from the use or application of the information contained herein. The techniques and suggestions are used at the reader's discretion and are not to be considered a substitute for veterinary care. If you suspect a medical problem consult your veterinarian.

The Leader In Responsible Animal Care For Over 50 Years!®
www.tfh.com

TABLE OF CONTENTS

1

HISTORY

of the Papillon

E
ven people who despise most other insects stand in awe of the
butterfly. Its delicate but vibrant wings and nimble flight patterns
can bring a smile to the face of anyone who is lucky enough to
encounter one of these spectacular creatures. The Papillon, named
after the French word for butterfly, shares many qualities with its
agile namesake. Both are instantly recognizable due to their most
prominent features. For the butterfly, these are its colorful wings;
for the Papillon, these are the beautifully fringed ears that make one
instantly understand how this breed got its name.

Like the dainty butterfly, the Papillon moves easily, whether walking on a leash
around his neighborhood or trotting around a show ring. This surprisingly athletic
little dog can also show off his fluidity by effortlessly navigating the obstacle courses
of agility competitions. Despite all his energy, however, the Papillon is considered one
of the most contented lap dogs, much to the delight of countless owners. Unlike the
elusive butterfly, the "butterfly dog" is both a free spirit and a homebody.

EARLY DEVELOPMENT OF THE BREED

The Papillon (pronounced pah-pee-yown) has one of the longest histories of any toy
breed, but details of the dog's lineage are often debated. Some fanciers insist the breed
originated in Asia, whereas others argue that it came from Belgium, France, Italy, or
Spain. Some even believe that the Papillon has Latin American roots, although this
is unlikely since the breed existed long before the conquest of Mexico, which is
evidenced by the dog's appearance in numerous Western European works of art,
including paintings by several master artists, such as Francisco Goya, Peter Paul
Rubens, and Sir Anthony Van Dyck.

Known for a time as the Dwarf Spaniel, the Papillon most certainly spent
at least a portion of its early existence in Spain. The word spaniel, after all,
means dog of Spain. It is doubtful, however, that this breed originated
there since the Spanish dogs of the era were expected to offer practical

The Papillon is a small, elegant dog, distinguished from other toy breeds by his large, butterfly-like ears.

function as well as beauty. Lap dogs were virtually unheard of in Spain at that time.

One of the more probable theories suggests that 12th century Italian merchants transported these little dogs in baskets on the backs of mules into other countries, where they were further developed. A great number of the breed's early European admirers were members of high society, particularly in France, the country best known for developing the breed and ultimately naming it.

The earliest Papillons did not have the butterfly-like ears that they do today. They originally had folded ears. The erect-eared dogs did not appear until the late 1800s. Today, the erect-eared variety is known as the Papillon, and the drop-eared variety is known as the Phalene, a French word meaning moth. Interestingly, the two varieties are often littermates and differ only by this one distinguishing feature. Most countries, however, judge the Papillon and Phalene as two separate breeds, even though the breed standards are nearly identical and the only difference is ear carriage. Only the United States and the United Kingdom judge them as variations of the same breed.

Many early Papillons and Phalenes were solid-colored dogs. Today, both varieties are parti-colored—white with colored markings. The most common of these are white with black, white with lemon, white with red, white with sable, and tri-color (white with both black and tan).

BREED HISTORY IN ENGLAND AND THE UNITED STATES

Although the Papillon was prized by many ruling families of Europe, the breed was not introduced into England until approximately 1905. The first English champion Papillon was born in 1922. His name was Gamin de Flandre, and he won his title in 1925. The Papillon Club of the United Kingdom was officially organized two years later. During the club's inaugural year, 17 Papillons were registered. Even with a limited amount of breeders, the number of newly registered dogs jumped to 64 the following year.

As with so many other dog breeds, the Papillon faced many setbacks as a result of the outbreak of World War II. Club activities and breeding programs alike were hindered by the war, although passionate enthusiasts helped the breed survive this turbulent period in history. Once the war ended in 1945, the club quickly resumed full operation, growing to 40 members by 1951. Although this total pales in comparison to the hundreds of members the Papillon Club has today, it was an impressive number at the time.

Recognition of the Papillon by the American Kennel Club (AKC) came in 1915, along with the first United States champion, Joujou, who was bred by Mrs. DeForest Danielson. In its early history in the United States, as in Great Britain, there were only a limited number of breeders, causing the Papillon's popularity to rise gradually. The Papillon Club of America (PCA) formed in 1930 and held its first specialty show in 1936. The winner was Mrs. Danielson's Eng./Am. Ch. Offley Black Diamond. Due to the faltering of the club, however, a second specialty show did not take place for almost two decades, when the club was reactivated.

a/k/a The Papillon

At different points in the Papillon's history, the breed has been known by several different names. These include:

• Belgian Toy Spaniel

• Butterfly Dog

• Continental Toy Spaniel

• Dwarf Spaniel

• Epagneuls Nains Continental

• Little Squirrel Dog

7

After dealing with some obstacles in the 1950s, the PCA forged on through the efforts of one of its most celebrated leaders, Catharine D. Gauss, a former vice-president of the club. She is credited with initiating a much-needed overhaul of the Papillon breed standard. Unfortunately, this important yardstick by which all show Paps are judged was again modified in 1968. This time the changes brought forth more altercation than celebration. First, liver coloring was deemed a quality worthy of disqualification. This led to a fair amount of confusion among judges because the color liver had yet to be adequately defined. Second, the generalized term "mismarkings" was also cited as grounds for disqualification, paving the way for every owner and his grandmother to find an embarrassing mismark on their beloved Papillons. Luckily, the third draft of the Papillon breed standard was again updated in 1975. The only colorations currently considered unacceptable by the AKC are entirely white and combinations including no white at all.

MEMORABLE PAPILLONS

Although the number of AKC-registered Papillons has been on a steady increase over the last decade, the Papillon

The Establishment of Kennel Clubs

When dog fighting was outlawed in the 1830s, dog shows developed as a way for owners to display their dogs in a more positive way. The first organized events of this kind occurred in England in 1859 and in Quebec, Canada in 1867. Without breed standards as guidelines, however, judging was problematic. The rules seemed to be different at every show, and with no standards for obedience within the ring, mayhem frequently ensued.

As a means of registering official standards for each breed, The Kennel Club (KC) of Great Britain was established in 1873. The American Kennel Club (AKC), founded in 1884, created basic rules for the show ring. The establishment of the Canadian Kennel Club (CKC) followed in 1888.

Today, kennel clubs are nonprofit organizations whose members work together to create and uphold standards for all dog-related issues, including the registry and showing of purebred dogs. Many such clubs exist in countries throughout the world, but the KC and the AKC remain two of the most prominent and influential.

Papillons are among the top toy winners in obedience, tracking, and agility.

remains one of the rarer US dog breeds. This hasn't stopped the butterfly dog from making strides in all kinds of organized activities. You will find Papillons among the top toy winners in obedience, tracking, and agility. One such dog, Ch. and OTCH Loteki Sudden Impulse, UDX, TDX, MX, is presently the most ACK-titled dog of any breed. Papillons are also among the most devoted therapy and personal-assistance dogs.

A Papillon named Ch. Loteki Supernatural Being became the oldest dog to win Best in Show at the Westminster Kennel Club Dog Show in 1999. He was 8 years, 1 month, and 10 days of age at the time. More informally known as Kirby, this record-breaking winner was also the first dog to win both Westminster and the World Dog Show in Helsinki, Finland. Another well-known winner, Tussalud Story Teller, won the Toy Group at England's distinguished Crufts Show in 1996.

INFLUENTIAL PAPILLON OWNERS

Papillon owners have included many aristocrats, including Madame Pompadour and Marie Antoinette of France, Queen Sophia Dorothea of Germany, and Queen Ann of Austria. In addition to these famous ladies, King Henri III of France also adored this toy breed, perhaps more than any other fancier in history. The monarch, who was known for carrying his dogs to court with him in baskets, even declared the breed the official dog of the Royal Court during his tenure.

It is interesting to note that even royals can fall victim to unscrupulous breeders. King Henri met one such person in Lyon, a 16th century opportunist who charged him exorbitant prices for the pups he desired. After spending more than 100,000 crowns on his passion for Papillons in a single year, King Henri began allowing his three favorite dogs to sleep with him and bestowed them with the regal honor of serving as his personal bodyguards.

On a fateful day in 1589, one of these dogs, a female named Lilene, accompanied the king on a trip to St. Cloud, where she tried to save her eminent master's life. Carrying false papers, a Dominican friar named Jacques Clement was granted permission to deliver his deceptive documents to the king. Perhaps sensing the impending danger, Lilene began barking at the monk relentlessly, to the point that the king remanded her to another room with her fellow Papillons. Once alone with the ruler, the friar immediately stabbed Henri. Clement might have escaped unnoticed if not for the dogs, who were still within earshot of the king. They alerted his staff who then apprehended the assassin. Henri's final words were said to be an expression of his regret for not heeding his dear Lilene's warning.

This was not the only Papillon linked with a notorious demise. Shortly before Marie Antoinette was executed at the height of the French Revolution, she was said to have brought

Hollywood "Faux Paws"

In the 2001 film The Affair of the Necklace, Hilary Swank plays Marie Antoinette, the infamous Queen of France who was beheaded for treason in 1793. Antoinette, a passionate Papillon enthusiast, was said to have walked to the guillotine with a Papillon in her arms. (The dog was fortunately spared the notorious monarch's fate.) In this movie about her life, however, there were no Papillons. Instead she was shown with a Chinese Crested, a dog breed that wasn't brought to Europe until many years later.

one of her two Papillons with her to the guillotine. Fortunately, the dog's life was spared. He and her other dog were subsequently cared for in her home, a building that still stands today in Paris—aptly named the House of Papillons.

The Papillon's popularity waned following this period of great social upheaval. Because the breed had been prized for so long by aristocracy, it had become a symbol of the high society that the populace was working so hard to transcend. Of course, Papillons eventually found their way back into the hearts of the French people, but this time the breed began showing up in both affluent and middle-class homes alike. By the 19th century, Papillons appeared in paintings not only by well-known artists but by fledgling painters whose work graced more modest walls.

CHARACTERISTICS
of the Papillon

One of the most obvious reasons people notice the Papillon is the plentiful ear fringe for which this "butterfly dog" was named. Consider the breed's compact size and graceful appearance, and one is hard pressed to find a more visually appealing companion. The only thing that in fact surpasses the Papillon's gorgeous looks is the breed's charming nature. Eager to meet new people and shower them with affection, the Papillon packs a lot of personality into his tiny posture.

C'EST MAGNIFIQUE!

If dog shows were beauty contests, the Papillon would surely win each and every one. The breed just has that special *je ne sais quoi* that *I don't know what*—that separates most other breeds from the more striking ones. Is it the ears alone that do this? Most fanciers would say this is definitely not the case. A well-bred Papillon has many beautiful features. It is the combination of these characteristics that makes the breed stand out from the crowd.

Body

Standing just 8 to 11 inches (20 to 28 cm) tall at the withers, the Papillon is slightly longer than he is tall. Dogs measuring 12 inches (30.5 cm) or taller are disqualified from competing in conformation. Although the breed standard designates no weight range, an average Papillon will typically weigh between 3 and 9 pounds (1 to 4 kg). The Pap, as he is often called, has a fine-boned structure. His weight is proportionate to his size; Papillons should never appear cobby (stout). Do not mistake delicate appearance and diminutive size to be indications of weakness, however. The Papillon is a hearty, energetic breed that is just as much a dog as his towering contemporaries.

Often called the "butterfly dog," the Papillon's generously fringed ears, which spread upward and outward like butterfly wings, are his most prominent feature.

Eyes

A Papillon's eyes are the foundation for his alert expression. Of medium size and dark color, they never bulge, but instead they draw you into his passionate presence. The rims are black, and the inner corners are on line with the stop, the skeletal junction between the back of the muzzle and the beginning of the topskull.

Ears

Inarguably the breed's most prominent feature, the Papillon's ears should be large with rounded tips. Set on the side toward the back of the head, they may be either the erect type or the drop type. The former variety, which spread upward and outward like a butterfly's wings, denotes a true Papillon. When in an alert position, the ears will each form a consistent 45-degree angle to the dog's head. Ears with this same shape but that point downward designate a Phalene, the drop-eared variety of this breed. A Phalene's ears must be carried completely down. Small or pointed ears are considered faults, as are those set too high on the dog's head or held only partially down. Having merely one ear in an upright position will also cost a Papillon significantly in the ring.

Head

Like the breed's body, the Papillon's head is small. The medium-width skull is slightly rounded between the ears, with a well-defined stop. Markedly thinner than the head and tapering toward the nose, the muzzle is typically one-third the length of the head. Slightly flat on top, the Papillon's nose is black, small, and rounded. Dogs with noses any color other than black are severely penalized in competition. The lips are black like the nose, thin, and taut. One does not see a Papillon's tongue when his mouth is closed in the standard scissor-bite, and either an overshot or undershot bite is considered a fault.

Topline

A Papillon's topline—the area from the top of the shoulder blades to the tail root—is straight and level. The dog has well-sprung ribs and a tucked-up belly. Accentuating the body, the tail is long and carried in a flowing plume. It may hang to either side of the body, but it should never be short, set low, or lack an arch over the dog's back.

Shoulders, Forequarters, and Hindquarters

The Papillon's well-developed shoulders should be laid back enough to allow easy movement. The dog's fine-boned forelegs should be straight and slender. Removing the dewclaws on the front legs is optional. The front feet are often described as hare-like—thin and elongated—and should not point inward or outward.

Like the forequarters, the Papillon's hindquarters should be well developed but also well angulated. Also slender and fine boned like their front counterparts, the back legs should stand parallel when viewed from behind. If hind dewclaws appear, they must be removed for conformation, and the hind feet should match the front.

Coat

The Papillon's abundant coat is long, fine, and silky. It flows across the body, lying flat against the back and sides with a

It Must Run in the Family

Papillons may receive more attention than their drop-eared counterparts, but fanciers of the Phalene consider this Papillon variety to be a rare gem. Phalenes, you see, may give birth to erect-eared dogs, but only Papillons with Phalene genes can give birth to a Phalene.

profuse frill of fur on the chest. There is no undercoat. Short hair covers the skull, muzzle, front of the forelegs, and from the hind feet to the hocks. The well-fringed ears are covered on the inside with silky medium-length hair. The forelegs are feathered on their backsides with fur that diminishes toward the pasterns, and the hind legs have what is called culottes, abundant fur covering the breeches. The hair on the feet is short with fine tufts appearing over the toes and growing beyond them, forming a dainty point.

Color

Papillons are always parti-colored (white with patches of any color or combination of colors). Any color other than white appearing on the head must cover both ears—both back and front—and must extend over the eyes without interruption. A distinct white blaze and noseband are considered a preferable addition to a solidly marked head.

Symmetry is also a highly desirable feature when it comes to facial markings. Size, shape, and placement of color patches are considered irrelevant factors. No one color or grouping of colors takes precedence over any other in judging, but a dog will be disqualified from conformation for either being all white or having no white at all.

FULL OF PERSONALITY

Even with all its good looks, the Papillon breed wouldn't be half as popular as it is today without its gregarious personality. This friendly breed may reel in its fanciers with its beauty, but it clearly keeps them coming back with its easygoing temperament. This is likely why many fanciers own not just one but two or more Papillons.

What Is a Breed Standard?

A breed standard is a detailed set of guidelines for the ideal physical characteristics of a particular dog breed. This description, which is used for both judging dogs in conformation events and breeding the best possible canine specimens, is typically created by the breed's parent club. It is a rare dog that flawlessly matches his standard, if such a perfect animal even exists at all. Interestingly, the breed standard for a particular dog in the United States may differ significantly from the standard for that breed in another country, making the judging of international shows an understandably arduous challenge. The most comprehensive breed standard is also open to at least a small amount of interpretation and personal taste.

Extremely intelligent, lively, and charming by nature, the Papillon packs a lot of personality into his tiny posture.

Temperament

A good fit for a wide range of human personalities, the Papillon disposition is neither shy nor aggressive. This is a confident dog who enjoys pleasing his owner, but he must be trained regardless of how small he is! It is the breed's tenacity, after all, that will help instill either positive behaviors that owners praise or negative actions that they ignore. Left untrained, a Papillon can become extremely spoiled, and this can hurt even the best relationship between a dog and his owner. It can also seriously limit the number of places you can bring your beloved dog. Teaching your pet at least a few basic commands will help him understand who calls the shots; it will also open the lines for all further communication between the two of you.

Extremely intelligent and highly trainable, the Pap can learn virtually any command or trick as long as it is broken down into easy-to-learn steps and taught in manageable stages. Papillons are regular participants in a wide range of advanced activities, including obedience, conformation, agility, and therapy work. Therapy work is in fact an ideal fit for this gentle breed, for

Papillons both want and need human companionship. They thrive when they are pleasing their masters and tend to be extremely empathic to their owners' moods. This positive attitude is a must for owners in the midst of training their pets. You may be surprised to know that Papillons are sometimes used as service dogs for people with certain disabilities. Despite their diminutive size, these bright little dogs can be trained to be the arms and legs of a physically handicapped individual. They can turn light switches on and off and even remove laundry from the clothes dryer! They can also assist people who suffer from psychiatric disorders by calming them in high-stress situations.

Many Papillons will sit contentedly in the laps of their owners for great lengths of time, making them superb pets for the elderly. They loved to be adored. Interestingly, though, these same dogs will also jump at a chance to run around a fenced backyard, chasing balls or other toys or playing with other dogs. Care must be taken, of course, when your Pap's pals are bigger than he is. Always in the moment, these little dogs possess a strong appreciation for all the different nuances of life. A Papillon seems to be up for either a quick walk or a long ride to virtually anywhere at any given time.

It should be noted that the only difference between the Papillon and the Phalene is physical appearance. Although fanciers who prefer one variation to the other may insist that their dog is sweeter or smarter, this is likely due to an owner's soft spot for that variety. Regardless of where their personal loyalties lie, most owners possess a strong appreciation for both the Papillon and the Phalene, but a certain amount of rivalry does exist between the two camps. Some Phalene owners even propose that Phalenes of equal or higher quality than the

Choose Miss Congeniality!

Although another dog may have better markings or other features that would make him stand out in the show ring, the Papillon with the most loving personality is usually your best bet when selecting a pet. An individual dog's looks can change over time, especially as he grows from a puppy into an adult, but his temperament will be one of his most deeply ingrained characteristics. Fortunately, most Papillon owners don't have to sacrifice beauty for an amiable nature, but never underestimate the value of a friendly personality. One of your dog's more breathtaking littermates might someday earn a championship in conformation, but your easygoing pup may acquire both obedience and agility titles due to his eager-to-please disposition.

Although the Papillon is a confident dog who enjoys pleasing his owner, he may exhibit problem behaviors if left untrained—despite his small size!

competing Papillons are often overlooked in the ring due to a judge's lack of experience with this lesser known dog.

Behavior

Papillons do have some traits you should take into consideration when determining how well this breed would fit in with you and your family. Just like other dogs, they may sometimes act in ways that their owners consider unacceptable, but many of these behaviors can be resolved with proper training.

Excessive Barking

Because Papillons form such strong bonds with their owners, excessive barking can sometimes be a problem if a dog is left alone for long periods of time. This can easily be prevented by bringing your portable pet along with you whenever you can and by providing him with plenty of fun distractions such as toys when you can't. Occasionally, a Papillon will suffer from

Before You Buy That Doghouse…

While most Papillons greatly enjoy spending time outdoors, this is not a breed to be kept outside most of the time. Your Papillon will jump at the chance to go for daily walks and play fetch in your backyard, but he will be miserable if you remand him to an expansive fenced area to spend time alone for long periods of time. He will also probably bark to the point of annoying anyone within earshot. For a Papillon, the biggest part of the fun in venturing outside is spending time with his favorite human.

outright separation anxiety. This is a serious situation for which an owner should seek the help of a veterinarian or an animal behaviorist.

Barking sometimes runs in Papillon families. When selecting a puppy, ask the breeder if a particular line is prone to this behavior. You can somewhat tell just by visiting with the dog's parents, but understand that nearly all Papillons will bark when seeing someone for the first time. If the barking continues long after you arrive, the behavior may likely be a challenge with one of this litter's pups. Spending some time with a Papillon in need of adoption will similarly help you make an educated guess as to whether the dog has a tendency to be "yappy." Training can often correct this problem, though, so don't let a little vocalization stop you from bringing home the dog of your dreams.

Housetraining Problems

Toy breeds are often stereotyped as being hard to housetrain. This is unfortunate because housetraining potential is considerably more dependent on an owner's dedication to the task than it is on the dog's breed. A friend of mine once asked for my advice in a problem she was having with the adult toy dog she'd had since he was a puppy. It seemed she was coming home from work each day to find at least one unwanted surprise on the bathmat in her master bathroom. When I asked how much time she had spent housetraining her dog, she admitted that she really hadn't worked very hard at the task. "He was so tiny when I brought him home," she confided sheepishly, "and I didn't want to expect too much of him, so I let him go in the bathroom. Now that I'm working long hours, I'm often away from home all day. He's so smart, though—I never even trained him to go on the mat, but he does it there every time." The truth was that my friend had indeed trained her dog to do exactly what he was doing by not taking him to an acceptable place to do his business right from the start. I suggested buying a litter box and redirecting him to go there whenever he needed to eliminate. Litter box or paper training is often best for anyone who works full time and has a small pet.

It is true that an individual dog's personality can affect training success, but consistency is the key to moving beyond any hindrances of this kind. The longer you wait to establish a schedule, the longer it will take your dog to succeed. Dogs, like children, have a way of living up (or down) to the expectations we set for them.

Adjusting to New Homes

Although Papillon puppies are generally quick to embrace new people, adopted pets may need a little extra time to adjust to their new homes. It can take several weeks for an adopted Papillon to become affectionate and fully interact with his new family. Whether you found your dog at a shelter or he had been staying with a foster family before being placed with you through rescue, he is likely missing his previous home and family. He will need your care and compassion as he acclimates to all the changes being thrust upon him.

Whenever possible, provide your Papillon with a toy or other item that bears the scent of his previous caregivers. This will help comfort him as he adjusts to his new life. Also, make

A happy and versatile breed, Papillons can thrive in a variety of different home environments and can be a wonderful addition to many households.

Worth the Wait

Because their litters are small—usually consisting of just two or three pups—Papillons are frequently spoken for long before a particular litter is even born. For this reason, you may have to wait a while for a puppy. Adding your name to a waiting list does not mean you are obligated to purchase a specific dog sight-unseen, but it will ensure that you will be next in line when one does become available. Your patience will be well worth the effort when you finally bring your precious Papillon puppy home.

a point of frequently petting and massaging him gently if he seems to enjoy it. Try to be patient. It won't take long before your Papillon will be showering you with kisses whenever he gets the chance.

Males Versus Females

As with many other dog breeds, Papillon temperaments can vary somewhat from one individual to another, especially between the sexes. Although both males and females can excel in the show ring, males are said to be a bit more easygoing and affectionate as pets. Females, even after they have been spayed, tend to be a bit more dominant in personality. Many breeders suggest starting with a male Pap and then adding either a second male or a female once the first dog has settled into your home. The premise here is that the male will likely accept a housemate of either sex without challenging him or her for the position of top dog. Many breeders also tell me that males frequently grow better coats, but don't tell those dynamic females!

Some Papillons can be a bit reserved around strangers, especially if they have formed an intense devotion to their owners. This too seems more prevalent in females. By socializing your Pap early, though, you can help her see that she doesn't need to be wary of strangers quite so much.

Adaptability

Papillons can thrive in variety of different environments. Owners from the Big Apple to Boise can provide these adaptable little dogs with everything they need. Whether your Papillon is a city slicker or a country dweller, there are a few things that you will need to do to keep your dog and the rest of your family safe and happy.

If you live in an urban area, for instance, you must make sure that your Papillon is not bothersome to your neighbors. While you might find your dog's voice to be music to your ears, the tenants in the apartment next door may perceive the sound as anything but soothing. Papillons are often the first members of their households to hear arriving visitors (or any other sounds), and they are remarkably swift at alerting their masters to these important matters. If you live in a building in which your Pap's watchdog aspirations could pose a problem with your neighbors (and subsequently your landlord), proper training is a must.

If you live in a rural area, traffic and noise will be unlikely problems for you, but contact with wild animals can create situations that are just as distressing. As we encroach upon the territories of these animals, even suburban neighborhoods are being confronted by unexpected visitors like coyotes, bobcats, and fishers. In addition to being common carriers of diseases like rabies, these animals can often kill a toy dog with just a nasty bite. This is why it is important to supervise your dog and provide him with a safe enclosure whenever he spends time outside and to leash him whenever you venture past your yard with him, even if no cars or sports utility vehicles are racing down your road.

Unfortunately, wild animals aren't the only outdoor threats to your Papillon. Always be on the lookout for larger dogs in your neighborhood. An overly zealous Golden Retriever may mean your Papillon no harm, but his imposing physique could seriously injure—or even kill—him if the bigger dog hasn't been trained to interact gently with smaller animals. Outdoor cats can also threaten your Papillon's safety because many of these street-smart felines rival your toy dog in size and attitude. I'm sure many dogs (even larger breeds) would prefer an encounter with a startled skunk to being on the receiving end of a testy tabby's claws.

Always supervise your Papillon around larger dogs who haven't been trained to interact gently with smaller animals.

COMPATIBILITY WITH OTHER PETS

When raised together, Papillons usually fare just fine with other pets. A few dog breeds, however, are not recommended for this kind of integration. Sighthounds such as Greyhounds, for example, may perceive your Papillon to resemble the tiny rabbits these dogs have been chasing for centuries—an instinctive habit that is difficult to break. Papillons are also considered incompatible with terrier breeds. Even the mellowest terrier has a strong instinctual prey drive, and just a single mishap could prove deadly for your petite pet.

NO KIDDING AROUND

Papillons adore children who treat them well, but most kids simply lack the maturity to understand how gently these little dogs must be handled. If you have preschool-aged children, it may be best to wait a few years before adding a Papillon to your home. Well-coordinated toddlers can pose a risk to a Papillon by merely navigating their newly discovered world. Sadly, many Paps currently in need of new owners began their lives in homes with children too young and rambunctious to respect the needs of this delicate breed.

Just as children can inadvertently hurt a Papillon, a Papillon too can hurt a small child by simply defending himself in a scary situation. A normal childhood event such as a temper tantrum could scare a Pap and lead him to bite. Although tiny, his teeth are no less sharp because of his smaller size. Caution

Children and Toy Breeds

If you have children, you may find that Papillon breeders are a bit hesitant to allow you to purchase one of their puppies. Try not to be offended by this because the breeder is looking out for her dogs' best interests in the same way you would for your child's. If you feel confident that your kids are mature enough for a Papillon, ask if you can bring them for a visit with a particular breeder. Often, a breeder's fears can be alleviated by simply meeting the entire family and seeing firsthand how younger members will interact with one of her dogs. If the breeder still has concerns about your children's ages, you may be able to place your name on a waiting list for a future litter, or you may ask for a referral to a Papillon rescue group where you may find an adult dog who would be a better match for your family.

Children must be taught how to properly treat a small dog.

must always be exercised when children and animals are in each other's presence—for everyone's sake.

Even school-aged kids under the age of 12 must be taught how to properly treat a toy dog, which means not picking him up roughly, especially by the legs. As your son or daughter gets a little older and learns more about your Papillon, he or she can gradually assume a more significant role in the pet's care. The trick is matching your child's role in each activity with your pet to his current abilities. This will help build both your child's confidence and your Pap's trust in this younger family member.

TIME AND ATTENTION

A Papillon is not the right dog for you if you work long hours or spend a large amount of time away from home—unless you plan to bring your pet along with you. Fortunately, this breed's size makes it a realistic option to do just that. Papillons are highly social animals; they thrive when they are surrounded by their favorite people and other pets. Even if you work a normal 40-hour week, consider adding a second Papillon to your home if taking your dog to work is not an option for you. Two Paps will find endless ways to entertain themselves while you are away, but you also must have enough time to devote to both animals once you do return home for the day.

Spending a sufficient amount of time with your Papillon doesn't mean you will no longer be able to go out to dinner or

Papillons aren't typical lap dogs; they enjoy being physically active and are quite energetic and athletic.

see movies with friends. Simply set aside a small amount of time at regular intervals, and make this time sacred. Every morning before you leave for work, for instance, take your Papillon for a fun walk. This is a great way to start your dog's day on a positive note and deplete some of his energy so that he will rest a bit once you leave home. When you return home, take 10 or 15 minutes to play with your dog. He will quickly begin to look forward to this enjoyable ritual. By showing your dog that you will always have time for him in your daily schedule, you will help make the occasions you must be away from home more bearable for him.

If you can't take your Papillon to work with you, try to include him in your outings as often as possible. Trips to the bank and the dry cleaner may be mundane tasks for you, but any trip that involves a ride in the car with you is the *crème de la crème* of excursions to your pet. A good friend of mine brings her Cocker Spaniel, Finnegan, along with her whenever she visits the local library. The staff is always thrilled to see them coming, and they lavish Finnegan with attention and treats whenever he visits. Of course, not all businesses welcome dogs, so always ask before bringing your pet inside. You may discover that a fair number of establishments will allow a small, well-mannered dog to accompany his owner.

A Papillon can get enough exercise in an average-sized living room, provided that his owner makes the effort to play with him every day. Chasing balls and squeak toys or playing an active game of hide-and-seek is good for both your dog's body and spirit. Making exercise fun is the key to holding your Pap's interest.

Avoid games such as tug of war, though, which pit an animal against his owner. Instead, foster behaviors that you wish to encourage in your pet. For example, when you play hide-and-seek with your Papillon, always allow your dog to be the seeker. Teaching your dog to seek you out is not only fun for him, but it also teaches your pet an important habit: In the event of a life-threatening emergency, you want your dog to come to you, not run away from you when you call him.

Papillons aren't typical lap dogs; they actually like to be physically active and are quite energetic and athletic. Taking your Papillon for frequent walks is an excellent means of providing him with the regular exercise his body needs. Be sure to maintain a reasonable pace for your dog's tiny legs, though, and limit the distance you cover to help prevent overexertion. Daily walks around the block should be fine, but jogging and traveling miles at a time are activities better suited to larger breeds.

In addition to helping your Papillon stay physically fit, regular exercise is good for his mental well-being. Dogs who exercise routinely are far less prone to numerous types of behavior problems, including inappropriate chewing, house soiling, and even aggression. Exercise time also affords owners ideal opportunities to bond with their pets.

3

PREPARING

for Your Papillon

Welcoming a new Papillon into your family is much like preparing for the arrival of a human baby. You may initially feel overwhelmed by a number of pressing questions. Should your puppy sleep with you or in another room? Should you buy him a collar or a harness? Will he need a crate? The answers to these questions will depend on your own preferences and perhaps even on your dog's individual personality. What's most important is that you have answered these questions and feel adequately prepared when homecoming day finally arrives.

PUPPY OR ADULT?

The decision of whether to purchase a puppy or adopt an older Papillon may seem difficult at first. A little groundwork, though, can help you decide which route is best for you.

Puppies offer many benefits, including that they have no deeply ingrained bad habits. The weeks puppies spend with their mothers and breeders is crucial, but when cared for properly, young Papillons quickly acclimate to their new homes. Paps are also quick learners, making training a fun and fairly easy task for all involved.

Let's face it, puppies are adorable, but they require a great deal of intensive care. In the very beginning, they need to eat at least three times a day and must be taken to their elimination spot every couple of hours. Housetraining, in particular, can take considerable time and energy on behalf of an owner. The key here is to look for a dog whose age best matches your individual circumstances and abilities.

Perhaps adopting an adult dog better suits your lifestyle.

Deciding whether you want a puppy or adult Papillon is an important decision.

There are two very common misconceptions about adopting a dog. The first is that you cannot find a purebred dog in an animal shelter. The second is that only adult dogs are available for adoption from shelters and breed rescues. Neither of these is accurate. Of the 6 to 8 million animals entering shelters each year in the United States, purebred dogs make up approximately 25 percent of the canine population. While a fair number of these dogs are adults, the average age of an animal entering a shelter is surprisingly just 18 months old.

Another widespread belief—equally erroneous—is that most dogs in need of rescue are in this predicament because of their unworthiness as pets. On the contrary, many dogs are surrendered because of circumstances in their owners' lives, such as financial hardships, relocation, health crises, or divorce. A potential owner may also worry about the health of a rescued Papillon, but most rescue or shelter dogs are in wonderful physical shape, as well. The only things they are missing are loving owners to care for them.

If you are looking for a loving companion, but lack the energy level to care for a vivacious puppy, an adult Papillon may be an ideal choice for you. As one breeder explained, this breed's activity level is much higher than most people think. Puppies, in particular, seem to have an unlimited energy supply. However, when not properly channeled, this healthy vigor can easily lead to behavior problems, such as housetraining issues, destructive chewing, and even aggression. An adult Papillon, while still reasonably active, will require much less play time than a puppy.

WHERE TO FIND THE DOG OF YOUR DREAMS

Once you have decided to look for either a puppy or an adult Papillon, your next choice will be where to find the best dog for you and your family. No matter what age dog you are seeking, you must know a few important things before beginning your search: How can you tell a reputable breeder from a less desirable one? What is involved in the adoption process? How can you be sure the dog you select is healthy?

Breeders

If you want a young Papillon puppy, your best resource is a hobby breeder. For those unfamiliar with this term, a hobby breeder is a person who is first and foremost a passionate owner. This kind of breeder will typically offer just one or two different breeds at the most, and litters will be limited to just a few a year. Because their dams are also beloved family members, a single dog will usually have only a few litters of puppies before being retired to full-time pet status. Moreover, breeding is rarely a hobby breeder's primary source of income, since they put their dogs first and the dear old dollar last. This doesn't mean that you won't pay a fair price for a puppy. Good veterinary care and a quality diet for both a mother and her puppies require a significant financial investment.

A hobby breeder's primary goals are simple: to produce puppies in good health, of proper conformation, and with friendly temperaments. While these admirable objectives are rather straightforward, there is nothing quick about the selection process. Only dogs who most closely match the Papillon standard are considered for breeding. For this reason, many

Papillon parents are current or retired show dogs. Additionally, any dog being considered for breeding is screened for the genetic problems most common to the breed, specifically eye and orthopedic issues. A breeder must have a clear understanding of genetic inheritance. Finally, even if a dog looks like a great candidate for breeding on paper, none of these highly coveted traits matter if the potential parents don't have pleasing personalities. Excessively shy dogs, aggressive dogs, and dogs with inconsistent temperaments should never be bred. The best way to predict the temperament of a puppy is to look at his parents. Like people, dogs look and act more and more like their parents with age.

The best way to find a hobby breeder is by word of mouth. Although the Internet has become a shortcut to seeking everything from law advice to lawn care, it is not the best place to start when looking for a dog breeder. Just like the Yellow Pages, the net can only tell you so much. Instead, go online once you have received a recommendation from a local veterinarian, humane society, or fellow Papillon enthusiast.

Another great way to find breeders is by attending dog shows, but do wait to approach a particular person until her dogs are done competing in the ring. Most will readily talk to you afterwards because discussing Papillons is usually a breeder's favorite way to spend free time. Although certainly not necessary, communicating by means of a website and e-mail address can be an excellent way to get a better feel for the way she does business.

If all a breeder wants to talk about is money, move on. Also,

Backyard Breeders

Avoid backyard breeders. These dog owners tend to lack essential knowledge and experience. They often decide to breed their dogs simply because they adore their pets and jump to the conclusion that they would likely produce highly desirable offspring. While many of these people may be well intended, their mistakes can lead to serious consequences. If you see advertisements for a variety of different dog breeds offered for sale all at the same phone number, this is a red flag that the person is almost certainly a backyard breeder.

Although a backyard breeder may offer AKC-registered litters, remember that any Papillon puppy whose parents were AKC-registered can possess this official pedigree. Unfortunately, backyard-bred puppies usually fall far short of the AKC standard and frequently lack the wonderful temperament for which this breed is known. Because these breeders are notorious for skipping important steps in the breeding process, many of their dogs also develop health problems that could have been prevented by better selection of breeding pairs.

beware of anyone who tries to "sell" you a puppy. A caring hobby breeder will ask just as many questions as you do because the top priority should be matching dogs with their best possible owners. Typical questions asked are:

- What breeds have you previously owned?
- How much time will you have to devote to a new puppy or dog?
- What other animals do you own now?
- Have you ever surrendered a dog to a shelter or rescue group?
- Do you rent or own a home?
- Do you have a yard?

You may even be asked to provide references or written proof that your landlord or condominium association (if relevant) allows dogs.

Many hobby breeders don't advertise their litters. Because Papillon litters are so small (typically consisting of only one to three pups), breeders usually have waiting lists for dogs. In light of this, you may likely need to wait a while for a puppy. Before you decide to fill out an application (yes, many breeders require this step), ask to meet the dogs who may ultimately become your puppy's biological parents. These dogs are the best indication of the looks and temperament of their future offspring. You may need to wait awhile to meet the parents, though, if the dam is currently pregnant because this is a very vulnerable time in terms of her health. If the breeder asks you to wait for a visit for this reason, it is an excellent sign that she is putting her dogs' health ahead of everything else.

Visiting a Breeder

You should be able to meet the puppies once they are between four and six weeks of age. The six-week mark is an especially important period in a dog's social development, so entertaining visitors at this stage is usually a positive step for the litter. Even if you single out your own pick of the litter during this initial meeting, though, the breeder may not agree to make him available for a few more weeks. Puppies are not ready to leave their mother until they are between nine and twelve weeks old and are consistently eating well on their own. As one AKC judge explained, "These are slow-maturing puppies. If they

Choose a breeder whose puppies look healthy and happy and whose facilities are well maintained.

were children, I would hold them back from kindergarten until they were six years old." A breeder may also wait as long as five to six months to make a final decision about which dogs are show quality and which will be sold as pets. (Many breeders keep their show-quality animals for both conformation and future breeding.) Try to think of all this waiting as an opportunity to make sure both the Papillon breed and the breeder are right for you.

When visiting a breeder, first and foremost, look for signs that show the dogs are much-loved pets. Even if the breeder specializes in show dogs, these dogs too should be considered a part of the family. Are there toys around? Are the dogs kept inside the home or in a separate area? The facilities where the puppies are kept should be clean and in good repair. The dogs should look healthy and well cared for and have room to move around and play. They should also have access to fresh water. Mutual love and respect should be obvious between the breeder and her dogs, and she should be able to share a lot of information about each puppy in the litter.

Trust your instincts, especially those that raise any red flags. Even if everything else about a breeder seems acceptable, if you simply don't seem to have a rapport with the person, this alone could be enough reason to keep looking. If you need advice down the road, your breeder should be the first person you contact, so wanting someone who is friendly and approachable is a reasonable expectation.

Breeder Documents and Contracts

Before you take your new Papillon home, the breeder should provide you with a variety of paperwork for him. In addition

Breeder Checklist

Before you acquire your Papillon, be sure to do your homework. It is beneficial for both you and your breeder to learn more about each other before you make decisions or sign an agreement on a dog of your choice.

A good breeder will let you visit and spend some time at her facility. She will guarantee that your puppy is in good health and free from illnesses. She will also require that you have your puppy neutered or spayed at the appropriate age, unless you have a show contract. Always demand a written sales agreement that describes all terms of the sale, including the breeder's health guarantee and the spay/neuter agreement.

Here are some basics to consider when evaluating a breeder or rescue:

- You may consider it an invasion of privacy, but a good breeder or rescue volunteer will not just drop a puppy in your arms and take a check. She'll ask you many questions about your home situation and may even want to speak with your veterinarian. Although these procedures can seem intrusive, a good breeder or rescue coordinator is looking out for the welfare of her dogs.

- A good breeder has a spotless kennel. The animals should appear clean, healthy, and well cared for, and they should be housed in clean, roomy kennels with fresh food and water.

- A good breeder will offer you a contract that clearly outlines your responsibilities in regard to the dog you are purchasing. Be sure to read it carefully and question anything you don't understand before signing it.

- A good breeder socializes her dogs. It's very important that young dogs be introduced to the kind of life and circumstances they will be expected to live in by the time they are separated from their mother and littermates.

- A good breeder will happily provide references from former buyers.

- A good breeder is knowledgeable about the positives and negatives of her breed (no breed is perfect). She also may show her dogs.

- A responsible breeder will have had her dogs tested for certain genetic problems and inherited diseases. She will show you proof that your dog's parents have passed these tests.

The breeder should provide you with a variety of paperwork for your Papillon before you take him home.

to a written pedigree, you should receive a health warranty of some sort. This document will state that the breeder will take the dog back within a certain time period (usually until the puppy reaches a specific age) in the event of serious illness. Although the breeder may offer you a choice of surrendering the pet and either receiving a replacement puppy when one becomes available or receiving a refund, most breeders will work with owners who wish to keep their pets. Typically, this paperwork should also list and explain the genetic conditions for which the set of parents have been tested.

You may also be required to sign paperwork stating that the Papillon will be returned to the breeder if for any reason you cannot keep him. Good breeders don't want their dogs ever to end up in rescues or animal shelters. They also don't want their dogs contributing to the unwanted pet population problem, so spaying and neutering are common stipulations in many sales agreements. Some breeders even demand that owners agree to a list of rules. The details can vary, but they commonly include commitments to always walk their dogs on leashes when in public and to attend a basic obedience class within a certain time period.

If you plan to show your Papillon, your breeder may give you permission to postpone sterilization until your dog is done competing in conformation (a show dog cannot be altered). Most purebred dogs, however, are sold as pet-quality animals. This means that they receive limited AKC registrations that preclude showing. Even if you are seeking a show dog, no breeder can guarantee that a particular puppy will become a show winner, so steer clear of any breeder who makes such promises. Many factors contribute to a Papillon's success in the ring aside from his pedigree. Other factors that affect how well a particular dog does in conformation can be his mood on a given day or an individual judge's preferences for certain qualities.

Technically, the responsibility of a breeder is limited to selling you a healthy purebred dog, but many Papillon breeders enjoy keeping in touch with the people who welcome their puppies into their homes, and they can be wonderful resources down the road for advice, moral support, and even friendship.

Adoption Options

There are two basic means of finding dogs available for adoption. The first is checking with your local humane society. The second is contacting a Papillon rescue group. Begin your search by contacting those facilities in your area. Even if there are no Papillons available at this very moment, many shelters will put your name on a list and contact you when one is surrendered. A shelter may also be able to refer you to a Papillon rescue group close to you, or you may contact the Papillon Club of America at www.papillonclub.org/rescue for a referral.

Papillon Club of America Rescue

One of the most important of all Papillon organizations, the Papillon Club of America (PCA) Rescue works to find loving and stable homes for displaced Papillons regardless of a dog's age, health, or temperament. Although certain dogs come to PCA Rescue with issues that make experienced adoptive owners a necessity, many of these Paps are the unfortunate victims of their previous owners' changing circumstances. Not only is PCA Rescue a great resource for finding a dog available for adoption, but it is also provides Papillon fanciers all over the country with an ideal opportunity to help animals in need. Visit the PCA Rescue website at www.papillonclub.org/rescue to download an application to provide foster care or volunteer in other ways. Adoption applications are also available at this site.

One thing you will not find through a shelter is a show-quality Papillon. All animals surrendered to humane societies are spayed or neutered before being placed in new homes to help prevent future generations of homeless animals from being produced. Because all dogs competing in conformation must be sexually intact, showing is therefore not an option for a shelter dog's owners. Dogs coming from shelters can, however, compete in agility, obedience, and a host of other fun organized activities.

Adopting a dog from a breed rescue is a very interactive process. Be prepared to fill out an application and meet a rescue volunteer for a detailed interview. Many organizations require a home visit before official placement is made. As intimidating as this may seem, don't be frazzled by this important step. A rescue's first priority is providing each dog with a loving, permanent home. One of the best ways to ensure this outcome is by screening potential owners in this most personal environment. All family members should be present at the time of the visit, including any animals that will be sharing your home with your new Papillon.

Certainly, not all adopted dogs come from their previous situations without any baggage whatsoever. Some may suffer from separation anxiety or may be fearful of people. Others may be best suited for homes where they will be the only pets. These issues can range from minor to severe, but a match can usually be made for nearly every owner based on the individual's level of experience and preferences. Because most dogs in rescue spend time with foster families before being placed, many problems are addressed and often corrected before they meet their new owners. Rescues typically also offer follow-up resources to help with any ongoing problems or new issues that may arise after a dog's placement.

It may take a little time to find the right dog for you, but you could spend even more time on a waiting list for a newborn puppy from a breeder—and miss out on an ideal Papillon that needs you right now. As one breeder told me, "Some wonderful Papillons have come through the Papillon Club of America Rescue and have gone on to become wonderful agility or obedience dogs and family companions. Lots of love, patience, and time are the ingredients to having success with a 'second-hand' dog. It's time well spent."

The Adoption Process

During the adoption process, shelter volunteers will interview applicants to make sure that they can handle all the responsibilities involved in dog ownership. Their job is to ensure the best possible matches for both the dogs and their new owners. Some of the routine questions asked include:

- How many people live in your household?
- What are their ages?
- Is everyone in favor of adopting a dog at this time?
- How much time will your dog spend outdoors?
- On a scale of 1 to 10, how much dog training experience do you have?
- How important is it to you that your dog gets along well with other dogs?
- Do you plan to participate in any organized activities with him?

These owner surveys are designed to give the counselor a clear picture of the kind of dog you want and the type of owner you will be.

You will have also have an opportunity to ask any questions you may have about the dogs you are considering. Here are some things to ask that may help you to make your final decision:

- What is the age (or estimated age) of the dog?
- Does the dog have any medical problems?
- What is the dog's temperament like?
- What is known about the dog's history?
- How many homes has this dog had?
- Is the dog housetrained?
- Is there evidence of any previous obedience training?
- Is there evidence of any previous abuse or neglect?
- Why was the dog surrendered?

You should always ask these and any other questions you may have in order to make the most informed adoption decision possible. Once you complete an application, it may be as long as week before you are approved and able to take a dog home. Expect to spend at least a few hours speaking with the shelter staff and meeting different dogs. If the dog you select has not been spayed or neutered yet, this also must be done before homecoming day. You may not even find the dog you're looking for right away. In this case, the shelter can contact you when more dogs become available. Most facilities admit new animals on a regular basis.

Source: The Happy Adopted Dog, *TFH Publications, Inc.*

PREPARING YOUR HOME FOR THE NEW ARRIVAL

Providing your Papillon with a loving home is only part of your responsibility as a pet owner. You must also take every measure to ensure his safety. Puppy-proofing your house is actually a lot like preparing a home for a baby. A toy breed's size alone makes many tasks involved in this process easier. Your dog cannot be hurt by something he cannot reach, after all. To remove all dangerous items from your dog's environment, you must know which ones may indeed be harmful to him.

Start from the ground up—literally. By looking at your dog's surroundings from his lower vantage point, you will see things you may never have noticed otherwise. Sharp corners or exposed nails on furniture, for example, can pose a threat to your dog's eyes. Small items unintentionally left underneath chairs and sofas can pose a choking hazard. Low-lying electrical cords and empty outlets are also extremely unsafe. Puppies are naturally curious creatures; they deem any item they encounter acceptable for their unabashed investigation.

You must also take measures to prevent your dog from escaping the safety that you create for him within your home. Open windows and doors (even those with screens) make it possible for your Papillon to venture outside, where a multitude of dangers await him, including other animals, traffic, and extreme weather conditions. When leaving an exterior door open for even short periods of time—to carry in groceries from your car, for instance—place your pet in his crate or behind a safety gate. Gates should also be used to block off stairways until your puppy is able to walk both up and down the steps comfortably. It is also important to let other household members know the importance of taking these precautions.

Finally, remember to safeguard your belongings from your Papillon puppy, as well. Although chewing the leather on your new sandals probably won't hurt your dog, it will likely take him mere minutes to destroy your shoes. Leaving items like these available to the whims of your teething puppy can also damage your relationship with him as you become more and more frustrated each time you discover another ruined possession. By simply making a point of putting your things where they belong, you protect your beloved canine friend from becoming your foe.

Dangers lurk everywhere, often in places you might never suspect. Constantly be on the lookout for anything that might pose a threat to your dog's safety. By doing so you just might save his life.

SUPPLIES

Although the list of things your Papillon will need isn't long, there are a few items you should purchase even before bringing your new pet home. Fortunately, most are relatively inexpensive and will last your dog a long time. The key is selecting the right supplies during that all-important first shopping trip.

Crate

A crate is by far one of the most versatile items you will ever purchase as a dog owner. In addition to being an invaluable housetraining tool, a crate is one of the safest places for a Papillon to stay when you are not at home or when you cannot

A crate provides a safe place for your dog to stay when you are not at home or when you cannot supervise him.

supervise him. For example, despite the temptation to allow your little dog to sleep on your bed during the night, he'd be better off in his cozy crate. Considering the height of most mattresses, he could be seriously injured falling from the bed during the night without your even realizing it until morning. Crating is also one of the best means of keeping your dog quiet while he is ill or recovering from a surgical procedure such as spaying or neutering.

A crate also serves as a wonderful car seat for your tiny pet, who, if not properly restrained, can be tossed around during the normal stops and starts of the vehicle. Sadly, breeders tell me that many Papillons have been thrown into the windshield and met with untimely deaths. Always remember to seat belt the crate in the backseat to keep it safe and secure. The day you pick up your new puppy, be sure to have a crate available to ensure him a safe homecoming.

While your dog's safety probably tops your list of reasons for adding this item to your shopping list, the crate has another important function: it gives your dog a space of his own. Although this breed likes nothing more than spending time with his favorite people, it is a canine fact of life that dogs regularly seek out quiet refuges. Because your Papillon is so little, the spot he may choose on his own—if not provided with a crate—could be rife with danger. Just think of all the places a small dog can fit: under furniture, behind computers or television sets with dangerous power cords, or even in places where he may be sat on or stepped on accidentally if a fellow household

member doesn't realize he is there. For this important reason alone, I strongly recommend having a crate—even if you never plan to close the door.

Too Close Quarters

Hold off on buying your Papillon a crate if he spent his early weeks of life at a puppy mill or if he was previously owned by someone who similarly used the crate as a means of neglecting or punishing him. Although dogs naturally seek out den-like places of their own, these special circumstances will make the crate an unlikely comfort to one of these dogs. Instead, purchase a safety gate to help with housetraining and to keep your dog out of danger when you cannot supervise him properly.

The cost of a crate for a Papillon is much lower than that of a crate for a larger breed, so you may even consider buying more than one for the sake of convenience. Because the crate is so small, though, toting it around with you wherever you go is highly feasible. When bedtime comes, for instance, place your Papillon's crate in your bedroom, where he can rest easily knowing you are right there with him. Remember, dogs are pack animals; they prefer to be near their loved ones whenever possible. If you visit a friend's house with your dog, bring the crate along in case he gets tired or you encounter other pets that may not be as wild about your dog as you are.

Selecting a Crate

There are two basic types of crates (or kennels): hard plastic and wire. Each has its own unique advantages and disadvantages.

Hard plastic crates require virtually no assembly—a huge benefit for someone like me with poor mechanical skills. Plastic is also easy to clean and more suitable for travel because airlines typically require a rigid-style carrier. Plastic crates also create instant privacy, an important factor if your goal is to provide a den-like environment for your dog.

Wire crates offer more gregarious dogs a 365-degree view of their surroundings. When privacy is preferred, a blanket or towel may be placed over the top and one or more sides. These kennels collapse for easy storage, but putting them back together can be challenging—especially, if like me, you detest the phrase "assembly required." Wire crates are also typically more expensive than plastic ones, but they can save you money in the long run if your dog is a chewer.

Crate Requirements

No matter which kind of crate you prefer, the most important consideration should be size, especially if you plan to use this item for housetraining. The best size crate for a Papillon is 24 inches long (61 cm), commonly referred to as a "small" crate by most manufacturers' classifications. Your Papillon should be able to stand, turn around, and lie down comfortably within his crate, but he shouldn't be able to walk from one end to the other. While you may be tempted to indulge your dog by buying him

Money Well Spent

Although your Papillon may appreciate a bed of his own once he reaches adulthood, you may want to postpone this purchase until housetraining and teething are both mere memories. A puppy will fare better sleeping on the padded liner in his crate or on a folded blanket you no longer use. These items can usually be laundered more quickly and easily than a conventional dog bed and won't be as vulnerable to the whims of an adolescent chewer.

a medium-size crate (just 6 inches [15 cm] longer than a small one), the extra space will likely be used as a makeshift bathroom. The reason crates work well in housetraining, you see, is that most dogs prefer not to urinate or defecate in the same area in which they sleep. This housetraining benefit is lost on most pups, however, when they are given just a bit of extra space.

You will also need a padded liner. These standard-sized cushions are available in a full array of materials and designs and make the crate a more comfortable place for your pet. Select one that is machine washable for easy cleaning. You may want to invest in more than one so that a clean liner is always available.

Food and Water Bowls

Your Papillon will need a set of dishes, but not just any dishes will do. First, your Papillon's food and water bowl must be the right size for your petite pet. Second, you must choose the best material for your dog. Some owners prefer ceramic bowls because of their attractive colors and designs, but pottery made for dogs can contain lead. If you choose ceramic dishes, opt for table-quality items made specifically for human use because these will not contain this dangerous element. Ceramic bowls are also more susceptible to breakage than other materials.

While plastic dishes won't break easily, they present a different type of threat to your Papillon, a condition called plastic nasal dermatitis. Caused by an antioxidant in the plastic, this condition can result in swelling, soreness, and even loss of pigmentation in your dog's nose and lips. Plastic dishes are also extremely vulnerable to chewing, a common habit among younger dogs.

For all of these reasons, I prefer stainless steel dishes for my dogs. This material is durable, easy to clean, and doesn't subject my pets to any health problems. I always keep at least two sets on hand for each dog, so that a fresh set is always available when another heads into the dishwasher. Having extra water bowls to place at various spots throughout your home is also a good idea—in the bedroom during hot summer nights, for instance. Dishes should be washed daily. Even stainless steel bowls can expose your dog to serious danger if bacteria are allowed to accumulate on the surface. Simply rinsing your Papillon's dishes is not enough. You must wash them with warm soap and water, and dry them completely before using them again.

Toys

Ask a child what she wants for her birthday, and you will be reminded instantly of the importance of toys. The same is true for dogs. You can buy your Papillon a fancy new leash or a

Toys provide excellent opportunities for exercise, mental stimulation, and interaction between pets and their owners.

fashionable sweater—and he may need both—but what he will get the most enjoyment from is a simple squeak toy. One might even argue that toys are more useful than they are indulgent. Toys provide excellent opportunities for exercise, mental stimulation, and interaction between pets and their owners. They help alleviate boredom, and they can even help circumvent problem behaviors that often arise during idle time, such as excessive barking or howling and inappropriate chewing.

For all their fun and practicality, though, toys must be safe for your pet in order for him to reap any of these benefits. When selecting a toy for your Papillon, examine it closely. Any item with ribbons, eyes,

or other dangerous embellishments that could get caught in your dog's throat should be avoided. While chew toys can ease the pain of puppy teething and reduce the buildup of plaque and tartar, avoid rawhide. This popular chew toy material has an uncanny knack of breaking into pieces small enough to create a gooey mess on your carpet but large enough to form a dangerous internal blockage inside your dog's digestive system. Hard nylon bones, such as those made by Nylabone, are safe choices, and they keep your dog's teeth healthy as well. For a special treat, consider a hollow rubber toy that may be stuffed with a tasty treat like natural peanut butter.

Of course, you should inspect the condition of all your dog's toys regularly and throw away any items that pose a risk to your dog's safety. Be especially watchful of squeakers. As one breeder told me, many Papillons consider themselves to be proficient hunters and will often disembowel a toy in order to "kill" the squeaker inside it. Although a stuffed toy may become a beloved buddy to your pet, also keep an eye out for tears in the fabric because synthetic wool, a common stuffing material, can also create serious medical problems if swallowed. The retrieving instinct also runs strong in the Papillon, making small balls and soft flying discs smart choices for this breed. Rope toys are particularly versatile because many dogs like to chew them as well as chase them. When shopping for any kind of toy, only consider items of the right size for your dog's teeny mouth, however, or you may find you have wasted your money on an item he won't use.

Playthings are always more fun for your dog when he has someone to play with him. Running around the backyard with his most treasured possessions and his favorite people is a Papillon's idea of paradise. It is also important to rotate toys often because these intelligent little dogs often get bored very quickly. If you don't provide toys that hold their interest, they will seek out other things to play with, most likely items they shouldn't.

Leash

Although toy breeds are certainly small enough for their owners to carry virtually anywhere, it is vital to remember that these little dogs are indeed dogs. Just like larger breeds,

A collar or harness must be properly fitted for safety and comfort.

Papillons delight in being able to investigate their surroundings. Important tasks like socializing your puppy are hard to accomplish if he is unable to meet his new friends in this up-close and personal way. Papillons also need regular exercise and should know proper leash etiquette, even if they will be spending most of their outdoor time in fenced yards.

Selecting a Leash

The most important consideration when selecting a leash for a Papillon is the weight of the material. Chain leashes are simply too heavy for the delicate necks of this tiny breed. Instead, choose a lightweight cloth or nylon leash in a length that will allow your dog to walk comfortably alongside you (6 feet [1.8 m] is usually ideal). Leather, too, can be a bit heavy for Papillons. Slip-style leashes, commonly called choke chains, are completely inappropriate for any breed. Remember, these are not always constructed of metal; many slip-style leashes are made of nylon, but it is the design of these leashes, not just the material, that makes them dangerous for your pet.

A highly versatile option is a retractable leash. This plastic-covered reel style can be found at most pet supply stores in a variety of lengths, many with ergonomic handles for maximum owner comfort. What makes this leash so unique is that an owner can extend or retract it as needed, using a variety of lengths within just a single walk. This may be especially useful if your walks include a mix of quiet neighborhood streets and high-traffic areas where a shorter leash is a must for safety. A retractable leash is also an excellent tool for training because it enables you to teach your dog to come to you without a second person's presence to ensure his compliance.

Collar or Harness

As long as your Papillon doesn't pull while walking on his leash, he should be able to wear either a collar or a harness, depending on your personal preference. Whichever you choose, this item should fit your dog well. If a collar or harness is too small, it can hurt your pet. If it is too big, your Papillon can wriggle his way out of it, which can be especially dangerous if an escape occurs while you are in a public area. Never guess your dog's size; always measure him. When measuring your dog's neck for a collar, always place one finger beneath the tape before recording the number. If you prefer a harness, also allow a finger's width beneath the tape as you measure the chest just behind the front legs.

Like your dog's leash, his collar or harness should be lightweight. Most are available in a variety of fabrics and styles. Again, cloth and nylon are the best choices, and matching leashes are usually available. If you will be walking your Papillon at night, reflective material is a smart option, as are battery-powered flashlight charms that can be attached to your dog's collar and set to blink whenever you head outside together in the dark.

Because a collar can catch on a variety of household items (even when properly fitted), many owners choose to remove it from their pets as a safety precaution once indoors. If you prefer to keep the collar on to ensure that your dog retains his license and other identification tags (escapes can happen when you least expect them), select a collar with breakaway technology. This simple step could literally save your dog's life by preventing strangulation. Removing your dog's collar before crating him, though, is always a smart idea.

Identification Tags

Every Papillon needs two kinds of tags. The first is his dog license; most states require that owners license their dogs. Call your local city hall to find out exactly what paperwork you need to bring with you when applying for registration. This typically includes a current rabies certificate. If your dog has been spayed or neutered, bring along confirmation of this as well because the licensing fee for sterilized animals is usually even less than the already nominal amount charged for intact pets. Your Papillon's license can help identify him in the event that he is ever lost, but this can only happen if you attach the tag to his collar.

An even better way to ensure that your lost dog finds his way back to you is by attaching an engraved identification tag alongside his license. Available through mail order catalogs and online, personalized identification tags can be purchased and engraved on the spot through self-serve machines at many pet supply stores. Include your Papillon's name and your name, address, and phone number. Like all other accessories for your dog, this item should be small, so if space is limited, remember that the most important piece of information is your phone number.

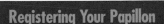

Registering Your Papillon

American Kennel Club: Registering your new Papillon puppy with the American Kennel Club (AKC) is easy. Your breeder should provide you with the necessary form, which will include both the dam's and sire's registration numbers, as well as your puppy's number. You just need to fill in your name and address, along with the name you have chosen for your dog.

Most breeders require that their kennel name precede the puppy's name. For example, if the kennel's name is Butterfly Kisses and you want to name your dog Smoocheroo, the full registered name would be Butterfly Kisses' Smoocheroo. The full name cannot exceed 30 letters. Spaces between words, apostrophes, and hyphens are counted in this total. You may choose a longer name for your dog's paperwork, such as Painted Lady, but use just Lady for her nickname.

There is a nonrefundable application fee for registration. You can mail this payment along with your completed paperwork to the AKC or register online at www.akc.org. There you will find detailed instructions, including a first-time user's guide and checklist for the organization's online registration service.

Kennel Club: In England, the complete registration of a litter with the Kennel Club (KC) is the responsibility of the breeder. During this process, the breeder will also officially name all the puppies. Each buyer is provided with a registration certificate for the puppy, complete with a section for the transfer of ownership that should be returned to the KC after the sale. A buyer should make sure that the breeder has signed this section of the document before completing the sale.

Microchipping

Although helpful, an identification tag has one inherent flaw: it can be removed very easily if your Papillon is ever stolen. In the past, owners who wanted a more permanent form of identification for their dogs elected to have them tattooed. This process, which involves applying a unique number onto the pet's skin using indelible ink, is very similar to tattooing a human. Unfortunately, even this seemingly permanent form of identification falls short of being infallible because it can be altered by an especially crafty thief.

A better option is to have your dog microchipped. A tiny device the mere size of a grain of rice is inserted under the skin between the shoulder blades. Whereas tattooing requires anesthesia (a step best avoided for Paps whenever possible), microchipping does not, and the entire procedure is as quick and painless as a vaccination. You must follow up microchipping by registering your Papillon's identification number with the proper company and updating your contact information whenever it changes. If you move far enough away to change veterinarians, be sure your Papillon's new vet includes this important number in your dog's file.

If a lost or stolen dog is found and brought to a veterinary hospital or humane society, he will be scanned for a microchip, which will tell them who to contact so that the dog can be reunited with his family.

Microchipping Compatibility Concern

Because microchips are changing along with the evolving technology used to create them—and because more and more companies have begun making these invaluable identification tools—not every scanner can read every chip. So how do you find out if your local shelter's scanning device can accurately read your Papillon's microchip? Stop by and see. If your dog's number doesn't come up, contact the chip's manufacturer and ask them to send your shelter a scanner, which they will often provide free of charge. Although the technology currently exists to make a universal scanner, competing companies must agree to share their technology to make this simple solution possible. Let your company know that as one of its customers, you see this as an important step in ensuring your pet's safety.

Even with this ongoing compatibility issue, microchipping remains one of the best ways for your Papillon to be identified if he is ever lost or stolen. In addition, though, you should always attach an ID tag to your pet bearing your name and phone number. This inexpensive item is frequently a lost pet's quickest ticket home.

Carrying Bags

Many Papillon owners like to carry their dogs with them everywhere. Although taking them along is rarely a problem, never having your arms free can be. For this reason, canine carrying bags have become relatively popular methods of transportation for toy breed owners. These bags offer ease of portability as well as safety. The sides are usually constructed with ventilated panels that have convertible coverings for privacy and cold weather. Unlike purses, they also come with padded bottoms, leash rings, and noncollapsible frames. They even offer such amenities as fashionable colors and pockets for your wallet and cell phone, so you have the option of carrying just one item.

Although virtually any bag will hold your tiny Papillon's weight, not just any bag will do. Allowing him to ride in your pocketbook can be dangerous for several reasons. Because your purse wasn't meant to carry a live animal, it has no openings for breathing when closed and poses the risk of your dog having a deadly fall if left open—hardly worth the cute look of having him peek out from between the bag straps. Using your purse will also expose your Pap to all the items inside of it. Your dog could easily be wounded with a pen, or he could decide to make a snack of your lipstick.

PET SITTING, DOG DAY CARE, AND BOARDING OPTIONS

According to the American Animal Hospital Association, 67 percent of pet owners say they feel guilty about leaving their animals home alone. If you spend numerous hours away from home each week, your Papillon may indeed start to feel lonely. If he has been trained to eliminate outdoors, he may also need to be taken for a walk long before you return home each day. In either of these situations, a practical solution is necessary.

If possible, take your Papillon to work with you. While there are many businesses to which you may not be able to take your dog, you will never know what your boss will say until you ask. With 62 percent of American households having pets, millions of other dog owners out there may be very open to allowing a *Take Your Dog to Work Day* each week. They just might not have thought of it on their own. Be sure to bring your Papillon's crate

If you are away from home often or can't take your dog with you when you travel, a qualified pet sitter or boarding kennel may be the answer.

with you, though, so you can place him safely inside it whenever you cannot watch him—and don't forget to bring his water bowl and some treats for your coworkers to offer him.

Another wonderful idea is speaking to your most trusted friends, family members, and neighbors to see if any of them would enjoy spending time with your Papillon when you can't. Like a loving grandparent to a small child, a retired dog lover may not want the awesome responsibility of caring for an animal of her own, but taking your dog for daily walks might add a little joy to afternoons that may otherwise be spent alone. Not only do pets improve a person's mental well-being by preventing loneliness and isolation, but they also offer benefits to physical health. The companionship of animals has been shown to lower a person's blood pressure and cholesterol levels and even increase survival rates in groups of patients who have suffered cardiac arrest. By asking for help, you just might be helping someone else in the process.

Pet Sitters

If you don't already know someone who can spend time with your dog, consider hiring someone. Pet sitters and dog day cares are available in most areas. Sometimes called dog walkers, pet sitters can be employed to feed and play with your Papillon, as well as take him for exercise and elimination, as this other name for their vocation implies. Because you must trust this person with both a key to your home, and even more importantly your precious pet, it is imperative that you interview candidates for this job with great scrutiny. Never assume that a high price guarantees the best service. Ask for references, and always follow up by checking them. (The best recommendations come from veterinarians and humane societies.) Include your dog in the interview process, and pay close attention to his reactions, as well as your own gut feelings toward a particular person.

Dog Day Care

If you would like to provide your dog with the company of other dogs, a dog day care may be an ideal option for him. Run similarly to day cares for human children, these businesses offer basic care, companionship (both human and canine), and also regularly scheduled activities (such as walks, games, and free-play periods). Most day cares group animals according to their size for the sake of safety, but there should also be a screening process for health and temperament.

When considering a particular day care, always request a tour of the buildings and outdoor areas. All facilities should be clean and well organized, and every staff member should possess an obvious love and respect for animals. At least one caregiver should be available for every 7 to 10 dogs. Ask how disagreements between dogs are handled; time-out rooms and other means of separation are acceptable, but punishment of any kind is not. You should also ask about the protocol for medical emergencies. If your dog is hurt, for example, is there a veterinarian on the premises? If not, to whom will your dog be taken? Just like a pet sitter, a day care provider should be someone you trust with your Papillon. If you find any red flags, keep looking.

Boarding Options

If regular travel is part of your job, or if you will be vacationing and unable to take your pet along, you will need to find reliable overnight care for your Papillon whenever you embark on a trip. Again, many times your best resources will be trusted friends and family members. If you find yourself without

such a person, a reputable boarding facility is another option. The selection process for this service will be much like that of a day care, with the obvious exception that

Bon Voyage!

The Humane Society of the United States recommends that you do not transport your pet by air unless absolutely necessary. Our beloved pets can face risks including excessively hot or cold temperatures, poor ventilation, scarcity of oxygen, and rough handling when flown in the cargo area of a plane.

Before you make plans to travel with your pet, follow these suggestions:

- If you plan to bring your pet on vacation, consider driving instead of flying. If this isn't possible, consider leaving your pet behind under the care of a pet sitter or a boarding kennel.

- If you are relocating across the country, consider using a company whose primary business is transporting animals.

- If you must transport your pet by air, your first decision is whether you can take him on board with you, which is your best option. If your pet is a small dog, most airlines will allow you to take him on board for an additional fee. To find out about this option, call the airline well in advance of your flight because there are limits to the number of animals allowed in the cabin area.

- When you contact the airline, be sure to get answers to these questions:

- Does the airline allow you to take your small dog on board with you?

- If that option isn't available to you, does the airline have any restrictions on transporting your pet as cargo?

- Does the airline have any special pet health and immunization requirements?

- Does the airline require a specific type of carrier? Most airlines will accept either hard-sided carriers or soft-sided carriers, which may be more comfortable for your pet, but only certain brands of soft-sided carriers are acceptable to certain airlines.

Remember, any inconvenience you might experience while researching and looking for safe travel options for your pet is minor when weighed against the risk of losing your companion forever. Above all, when making travel decisions, please consider what is best for your pet.

(Courtesy of the Humane Society of the United States)

A great way to provide your dog with companionship is by adding a second Papillon to your home.

your pet will be spending a longer, continuous period of time with these important caregivers during your absence. Be sure that your dog will receive regular opportunities for exercise and elimination each day, and don't forget to provide the staff with all the items necessary for your dog's stay—including his regular food, familiar toys and bedding, and any medications he will need during this time.

Two's Company

These fun-loving little dogs typically delight in spending time with their fellow breed members. Whether you have one or two dogs, however, it is important to note that increasing the number of dogs in your household also increases the amount of money you will spend on everything from dog food to veterinary care. And even if you hire a pet sitter to look in on your new twosome, you must have enough time and energy for both dogs at the end of the day.

Chapter

4

FEEDING

Your Papillon

ew things have a greater impact on our dogs' health than what we choose to feed them. A healthy diet keeps a dog looking and feeling good, it strengthens his immune system, and it can even help a sick dog heal faster. Because a toy breed like your Papillon consumes so little food compared to his larger canine counterparts, it is even more important that he eats a well-balanced diet designed specifically for his unique nutritional needs.

FOOD FOR THOUGHT

Deciding what to feed your Papillon may at first appear like an intimidating task. At times, it seems as if there is a new brand of dog food on the shelves each time I visit my local pet supply store. One such store in my area even presents a seminar to help its customers learn about basic canine nutrition and decide which food brands and formulas are best for their dogs. If your local retailer offers such a class, I highly recommend attending. Always listen with a discriminating ear; the more you learn about canine nutrition, the easier your feeding decisions will be.

COMMERCIAL FOODS

Commercial prepackaged foods are the most common choice among dog owners for many reasons. These foods are readily available, stay fresh for long periods of time, and save you the trouble of intricate menu planning. Just because a particular food works well for one dog, however, doesn't mean that it is best for yours. Your dog's dietary needs can be just as individualized as your own. Fortunately, a number of prepackaged options are available, making it possible for you to find the one that suits your Papillon best.

The best way to be sure you have selected a healthy food for your dog is to take a close look at the information provided on the package. Just as you would read the label of any new food you consider buying for your human family members, inspect your dog's food labels just as carefully. Because your Papillon

A well-balanced, nutritious diet will help your dog look and feel his best.

will be eating this food each and every day, it is perhaps even more important that you know what's in it. Never assume that a high price guarantees quality. Many so-called premium foods aren't at all superior to others when it comes to appropriate nutrition.

Ingredients List

Begin by reading the ingredients list. By law, dog food ingredients must be listed in descending order according to weight. This means that the first item listed should be the most prevalent, but some companies try to mislead consumers by listing many similar ingredients (grains, for example) individually. This pushes a less prevalent ingredient (such as chicken) to the top. Most dog owners would prefer a food made mainly of chicken over one made predominantly of grains. In addition to being less nutritionally efficient, many grain-based foods use soy protein, which may cause excessive flatulence (gas).

Even when a food's primary ingredient is a healthy meat like chicken, consider how much of the food's weight is made up of water—nearly 75 percent. A food made with chicken meal is actually the better choice for pets. Chicken meal is ground chicken meat with the water removed. Pound for pound, the nutritional value of chicken meal is superior to plain chicken. The same is also true for foods made from lamb or beef ingredients.

Bone meal and by-products, on the other hand, are not desirable ingredients. The former is more of a filler ingredient than a nutrient for your dog and in large quantities may be difficult for your Papillon to digest. By-products are those parts of animals not normally eaten by people, such as beaks and feet. They may even come from diseased animals.

Preservatives

One thing that all prepackaged foods have in common is preservatives. People have been programmed to think that the word "preservative" itself is bad. The reality is that without preservatives a food would have virtually no shelf life. The key here is choosing a food with safe preservatives.

Synthetic preservatives such as butylated hydroxyanisole (BHA), butylated hydroxytoluene (BHT), and ethoxyquin have come under extreme scrutiny in recent years. Studies have shown that high levels of BHA can cause tumors in the forestomachs of rats, mice, and hamsters. Because no data have

AAFCO Nutritional Standards

Deciding what to feed your dog can be a bit overwhelming at first, but fortunately an organization exists that puts a stamp of approval on pet foods that have been proven to meet a pet's nutritional requirements. This organization, called the Association of Animal Feed Control Officials (AAFCO), sets nutritional standards based on research and study for both pets and farm animals, and also maintains a list of ingredients approved for use in different types of animal feed. Although dog foods aren't required to meet AAFCO standards, reputable companies choose to meet them voluntarily. Basic AAFCO nutritional requirements are minimums: 18 percent protein and 5 percent fat.

If a dog food meets AAFCO standards, it can include the following statement: "Formulated to meet the AAFCO Dog Food Nutrient Profile for All Life Stages." (Puppy foods and foods made for a specific life stage have slightly different wording to reflect this.)

AAFCO makes it easy to determine if a food is nutritionally sufficient for your Papillon, and any food you choose should have this AAFCO statement.

Dry foods provide the most popular and diverse meal base for dogs.

been collected relating to animals lacking a forestomach, and dog foods contain such a minute percentage (0.02 percent of the fat content only), the FDA currently allows the use of these preservatives in dog foods. Although reliable data on ethoxyquin have been limited, sufficient concern has emerged for the FDA to request that dog food companies lower its levels in their products.

Tocopherols, on the other hand, are vitamin-based preservatives. Foods preserved with tocopherols have a shorter shelf life—especially once a package has been opened. But this is a situation where good health should take precedence over convenience. Just think of all the space you'll be saving by not buying in bulk.

Finally, before carrying that bag or can to the checkout counter, look for two very important numbers: the food's expiration date and the company's phone number. When I buy food for my family, I always check the dates and select those products that will last the longest. By doing the same thing at the pet supply store, I ensure that I am buying the freshest food possible for my pets, as well. If your dog doesn't consume all his food before that expiration date comes, buy a smaller package next time. If you want to save money, ask if your pet supply store offers a frequent buyer program. Many manufacturers and retailers provide customers with a free bag of dog food after a certain amount has been purchased.

If you have any questions about the food you have chosen, pick up the phone or go to the company's website, which is also typically listed on the package. I recommend clipping the label off and keeping it handy for this purpose. It is also vital that you have the identification numbers of your pet's food in the event that the product is recalled, so be sure to rotate the saved labels whenever you buy new food.

Dry Foods

By far the most popular choice, dry foods (or kibbles) are also the most diverse. They are usually highly cost effective, they require only minimal preparation, and owners need not immediately retrieve a dish containing uneaten food for fear of spoilage. Munching this hard food also helps keep your dog's teeth clean. Most brands offer varieties made specifically for toy breeds. These special formulas are not only made with your smaller dog's nutritional needs in mind, but they also come in easy-to-eat bite-sized pieces for your dog's smaller mouth. (If your older Papillon has lost a significant number of teeth due to decay or extraction, however, kibble might not be the best choice.)

To keep dry food fresh, store it in a sealed container once the package has been opened. Never merely rip open the bag and scoop out the food at meal time because this will cause it to go stale. Also, refrain from emptying a new bag of kibble into your container on top of even a small amount of food left over from the previous bag. Fat from the food can settle to the bottom and spoil when left too long. Instead, wash and dry the container thoroughly before adding food from the new package.

Canned Foods

Canned foods are also a popular choice among dog owners. They can be purchased just a few meals at a time or in larger quantities—and most dogs love it. Dogs have fewer taste buds on their tongues than people do. This trait has allowed larger dogs to eat for survival through the centuries. Toy breeds, however, have evolved under much less harsh conditions and as a consequence of this good fortune, they tend to be more

Eat, Drink, and Be Hydrated

If your Papillon's diet consists primarily of kibble, be sure his water bowl is kept full. Dogs who consume dry food generally require more water than those eating other types of food.

Papillons eating dry food may need their teeth brushed less frequently than dogs consuming wet food, but remember that brushing will be required whether your dog eats canned food or kibble. No food can replace regular dental care.

selective about the foods they eat. (Females are twice as likely to have a highly discriminating palate.) The pleasing aroma and taste of wet food is usually a great way to win over even the most finicky eaters. No matter how nutritious a food may be, after all, it can't do your Papillon any good if he won't eat it. A quality wet food is also every bit as nutritious as the same brand of kibble, but Papillons fed a wet diet must have their teeth brushed regularly because plaque and tartar form so quickly on their teeth.

When feeding canned food, always cover and refrigerate any unused portions to prevent spoilage. Allow some extra time when feeding these leftovers, so the food can warm to room temperature before being eaten. You may even choose to heat your dog's food for a few seconds in the microwave. Cold foods can cause stomach upset. Dogs with extremely sensitive tummies may even vomit from eating food served immediately upon being removed from the refrigerator.

Owners may notice that a dog fed a canned diet produces looser stools than his kibble-munching counterparts. This may or may not improve over time. Sometimes the addition of some roughage to his diet, such as dry treats, may help.

Semi-Moist Foods

A semi-moist diet may seem like the perfect compromise between wet and dry food. Most dogs quickly devour these yummy foods, which are typically sculpted into attractive burger shapes. However, this medium is anything but middle of the road when it comes to the excessive amount of sugar these foods contain. In addition to being bad for your Papillon's teeth, most semi-moist foods can be especially dangerous for dogs with diabetes or weight problems (a risk factor for the disease).

If you think your dog would enjoy the taste benefits of a semi-moist diet, but the excess sugar doesn't appeal to you, a healthy alternative to mainstream options is something called a dog food roll. Packaged similar to salamis, these foods offer a true compromise—pleasant taste and good nutrition. As with any type of food, though, you must check the label to make sure the brand is nutritionally sound.

HOMECOOKED FOODS

Sometimes it is our very language that stands between our dogs and their ideal diet. The words "people food," for instance, have long served as such a hindrance. This everyday expression is used to designate the invisible line between food manufactured specifically for pets and what we ourselves eat. The premise of this common philosophy is simple: Dog food is for dogs; people food is for people. If your diet consists mainly of high-fat dishes laden with salt and sugar (and low in vitamins and minerals), then your dog's kibble is certainly more suitable for him than that frozen entrée spinning around in your microwave. If, on the other hand, your typical meal is made with leafy green vegetables and lean cuts of meat, sharing your people food with your Papillon might benefit his health more than it hurts it.

Indeed, feeding people food to animals has been blamed for a number of canine health problems—obesity, diabetes, and tooth decay just to name a few. The real issues here, though, are overfeeding, poor menu selection, and lack of dental care. The fact of the matter is that owners can often provide their dogs with a healthy diet (and avoid many suspicious preservatives) by sharing a shopping cart with their dogs. Providing a homecooked diet, when done properly, is one of the best ways to make sure your Papillon is getting all the nutrients he needs.

Vegetarian Dogs

If, like millions of other people, you are a vegetarian, you may find yourself facing a bit of a dilemma when it comes to feeding your dog. Whether you choose not to eat meat strictly for health reasons or because you take issue with the concept itself (or you are moved by a combination of these driving forces), you may prefer that your dog also consume a meat-free diet. But can a dog be a healthy vegetarian?

While cats are true carnivores, dogs are omnivores; they do not truly need meat in their diets. If your dog doesn't eat meat, though, you must be certain you are providing him with an adequate amount of important nutrients like protein and iron. Talk to your veterinarian about selecting a prepackaged vegetarian food or cooking vegetarian meals for your pet at home. The variety of vegetarian regimens available from dog food manufacturers is constantly expanding. Still, you may need to offer certain supplements to cover all your dog's nutritional bases, whether you buy his food or prepare it personally.

Your vet may also advise you to wait until your Papillon reaches a certain age before transitioning him over to an exclusively vegan plan (a diet void of all animal products). Puppies need a certain amount of calcium and amino acids for proper growth. Once you make the change, you must also make sure your dog is thriving on his new vegetarian or vegan menu. Weight loss (even a small one) or changes in your dog's coat texture or mood are signs that some nutritional changes are necessary.

A carefully designed home-cooked diet can have many advantages for dogs with special needs, such as food allergies or certain medical conditions.

The biggest difference between our dog's dietary needs and our own is that dogs need more fat than we do. The canine body burns fat at an impressive rate, instead of storing it as the human body does. Just like us, our dogs also need water, protein, and a wide variety of vitamins and minerals to fuel their bodies' systems and remain healthy. They also benefit from the long-term energy provided by carbohydrates. Also like people, dogs gain weight when the number of calories they consume each day exceeds the total they burn. This makes a balanced diet a necessity. Unlike us, though, they don't care whether their food is seasoned or not, and in most cases they are better off without the spices.

Of course, certain human foods should never be fed to dogs. Onions, for example, can cause anemia. Chocolate contains theobromine, an alkaloid that dogs metabolize very slowly, making it poisonous to them. Although larger dogs may be able to tolerate a small amount of chocolate, just a small amount eaten by a toy breed could prove fatal. Among other foods not recommended for canine consumption are macadamia nuts, grapes, raisins, and any foods or beverages containing caffeine or alcohol. Dogs are also lactose intolerant, so milk is an unwise choice for them, as well. The only beverage you should give your Papillon is water.

Feed fresh fruits and vegetables whenever possible. If you cannot find a particular food in your grocery store's produce section, head to the freezer aisle. Canned foods, however, are too high in salt and sugar to be a healthy option. Also, skip the butter on your dog's servings to avoid unnecessary fat and calories.

Cooking for your pet may sound like an expensive and time-consuming undertaking, but when done right, it can be a surprisingly economical and straightforward process. By shopping the sales and feeding your dog many of the same meals the rest of your family is eating, you might not even notice the minimal extra effort you have to put into the preparation—like skipping the onions or the salt in your recipes. When considering cost, remember also that your Papillon's portions should be small.

For dietary information and specific feeding amounts, discuss homecooking with your veterinarian. She can help you make sure you are including all the important nutrients your dog needs—and maybe even recommend a good doggy recipe book.

RAW DIETS

Feeding raw food has become extremely popular with a considerable number of veterinarians and breeders in recent years. Based on the premise that raw foods retain the natural enzymes and antioxidants that are destroyed by the heat processing of prepared foods, the BARF (a frequently-used acronym standing for bones and raw food) diet consists not only of raw meats and bones, but also raw fruits and vegetables. Owners of dogs fed this way insist the results are obvious—shinier coats, cleaner teeth, and improved health.

This kind of plan is especially popular with larger breeds. The smaller digestive systems of toy breeds, however, put Papillons and other dogs their size at an increased risk of bones becoming lodged in their intestines. Chicken bones are of particular concern because they can be extremely small and are known for their splintering qualities. Bones can also cause broken teeth, which can have a whole range of effects on your dog's eating habits.

Although feeding boneless cuts of chicken or beef may not pose any threats in terms of blockages or broken teeth, it is important to remember that our dogs are not immune to the dangers of bacteria such as *Salmonella* and *E. coli*. While it is true that the canine digestive system is designed to accommodate raw meat, this again is an area in which the Papillon's petite size places him at a disadvantage. While a larger dog may merely experience a nasty case of diarrhea after coming into contact with contaminated meat, a toy breed is likely to suffer a more serious reaction, including death. The virus that causes

Hold These Fruits and Veggies, Please!

Avoid feeding your Papillon foods rich in oxalic acid, such as spinach, swiss chard, rhubarb, star fruit, and beets. This chemical compound interferes with calcium absorption, and in high concentrations it can cause stomach irritation and kidney problems. Healthy alternatives in a homecooked diet include apples, peas, carrots, green beans, broccoli, and zucchini.

Aujeszky's disease, a deadly illness also known as pseudorabies, is transmitted primarily through raw pork. These are just some of the reasons the American Animal Hospital Association (AAHA) recommends that pet owners not feed their pets a raw-meat-based diet.

If you would like your Papillon to reap some of the benefits of a raw food plan, but you are not comfortable with all the risks, consider feeding just the foods that pose no dangers as supplements to a prepackaged or homecooked diet. Raw carrots, for instance, are extremely rich in beta-carotene, a nutrient that helps maintain good vision and a healthy coat. It can even help stimulate appetite. Munching raw carrots helps exercise a dog's jaw and clean his teeth and gums, but your Papillon's tiny mouth may be better suited to eating grated carrots. Additionally, because dogs—even small ones—tend to gulp their food more than chew it, foods like carrots often pass through the canine digestive system without releasing the most nutritious substances within these vegetables. Grating helps ensure that your dog is receiving the most healthful qualities of the food.

PUTTING A FEEDING PLAN INTO PLACE

Deciding what to feed your Papillon is only one of the important choices you will make for your dog's nutritional well-being. How often you feed your pet will also have a significant impact on him. Should you schedule your dog's meals, or leave food available to him at all times? If you do schedule feedings, how many is the right number? Should this change as your dog ages?

In general, puppies need to eat more frequently than adult dogs—typically three or four times a day as opposed to just once or twice. With many other breeds, at least one of these meals is usually eliminated as the dog nears adulthood. In the Papillon's case, however, it is wise to keep feeding small amounts more frequently to avoid problems caused by low blood sugar.

Free Feeding Versus Scheduled Feeding

Free feeding, or leaving food available to your dog at all times, can be problematic at any age, but this is especially true for dogs at either end of the age spectrum. Owners must be certain that

Feeding Time!

Puppies Up to Four Months	Puppies Between Four Months and One Year	Adult Papillons (1 to 12 years)	Senior Papillons (Approximately 10 Years and Older)
Younger puppies need more protein than older dogs. They also need to eat more frequently. Feed your new Papillon puppy three to four times a day, dividing the total amount of food given among these meals. Offer water with each meal, but while you are housetraining, be sure to remove it about an hour or two before bedtime.	Once your Papillon puppy reaches four months of age, eliminate one or two of his daily meals. Somewhere between the ages of six and nine months, your pup should be switched to an adult food. Although larger breeds aren't ready for this transition until they are between one and two years old, smaller breeds reach their adult size well before this time, thus requiring less protein. As soon as housetraining is complete, you can also begin offering water at all times.	Most adult Papillons should eat two meals per day. Look for diets specially formulated for smaller breeds. Not only will these regimens contain the specific combination of nutrients your Papillon needs, but the food will also be sized more appropriately for your smaller dog's mouth than standard diets. You can offer variety in the form of healthy snacks like raw vegetables. Just be sure to watch your dog's weight because metabolism slows with age. Superfluous pounds will only be harder to lose as your Papillon approaches his senior years.	The senior Papillon's diet is perhaps the most individualized of all age groups. If your dog has any health concerns, your veterinarian may recommend feeding a specialty diet. If your dog is in good health, he may need a change of some other sort to renew his interest in eating. Wet food or homecooked food can often help with this. Because a Papillon's nutritional needs (and metabolism) change once again at this time, changing to a food made specifically for seniors is a good idea. You may also want to discontinue feeding harder foods if your dog's teeth are in poor shape or if he is missing teeth.

Your Papillon may need to eat a little more during the winter when the weather turns colder. Likewise, his appetite can wane a bit when summertime temperatures soar. If this happens, don't panic, but do make sure he is eating at least some food at each meal. Provide him with plenty of cool water to keep him hydrated, and avoid taking him outside during the hottest times of the day. If your dog stops eating entirely, contact your veterinarian immediately, as this is a sign of serious illness.

their younger Papillons are getting adequate nutrition for proper growth. This can be difficult when they aren't certain when or how much their dogs are eating. An erratic feeding plan like this can also make housetraining significantly more challenging. An older dog faces an increased risk of many illnesses, so being aware of any changes in your senior Papillon's appetite can help alert you to a problem before it intensifies. This too can be tricky for the owner of a free-fed dog.

An adult dog may do fine on a free-feeding plan, but bear in mind that changing back to a schedule takes far more time and effort than switching from a routine to free feeding. If the plan you have chosen is working for you and your dog, there should be no reason to make a change. If you find yourself in the midst of trying to bring the routine back, though, be patient. Divide the amount of food your dog is eating each day into several equal portions so that servings may be offered at various times.

If your Papillon refuses to eat, resist the temptation to leave his bowl out until his appetite returns; an average meal should last only about 10 minutes. You must be consistent in offering food again at the next interval, however, to avoid having your dog's blood sugar drop. Papillons and other toy breeds are highly susceptible to hypoglycemia (the technical name for this problem), and going long periods of time without food only heightens this risk.

FEEDING A PUPPY

A Papillon puppy needs to eat food made especially for his growing body. Servings should be given at least three times a day to keep his tiny stomach full. Puppies, in general, need a higher percentage of many nutrients (such as protein, fat, and calcium) than adult dogs, but this is especially important for toy breeds.

Because toys also have a higher metabolic rate and reach maturity faster than bigger dogs, owners of Papillons should transition their pets to an adult feeding plan earlier than the typical one- or two-year mark recommended for most other breeds. Many veterinarians recommend this change around the time you have your dog spayed or neutered. If you choose to do so, this is also the time to eliminate your dog's midday meal, instead dividing his food into two daily servings.

FEEDING AN ADULT

The transition to an adult diet presents an excellent opportunity for you to select just the right feeding plan for your maturing Papillon. The primary difference between commercial puppy formulas and adult foods is the amount of protein they contain. Though still an important nutrient, protein will make up a smaller percentage of your adult Papillon's diet. Generally, many more varieties of adult foods are available. In addition to choosing between ingredients like chicken or lamb, for example,

The Right Time and Place for Meals

If you have multiple dogs, it is a good idea to separate them during scheduled feeding times to ensure that each animal is indeed eating his own food. Many owners prefer feeding their pets in their crates for this reason. Wherever you choose to serve your dogs' meals, you must be certain that each of your pets is getting the right type and amount of food that is best for him. Free feeding can make this nearly impossible.

you must now also decide if your Papillon needs a food that will help maintain a healthy weight or keep tartar from accumulating on his teeth.

No matter which food you ultimately decide is best, a gradual changeover should be made. During the first week on the new regimen, replace just 25 percent of your dog's puppy formula with his new food. You can then replace 50 percent the second week, 75 the third, and so on until the change is complete. This will help prevent stomach upset and diarrhea, as well as help your dog acclimate to any major differences in taste or food texture.

If you adopt an adult Papillon, find out what kind of food he has been eating before you bring him home. While you may wish to ultimately switch him to a different regimen, it is wise to wait a while before doing so. Give him some time to adjust to his new home before adding another change to his life. Postponing this step just a few weeks can help make the entire acclimation process easier on your pet. Once he has settled into his new home, you can start transitioning him to the food you prefer he eat.

Some vets recommend changing foods from time to time to help ensure that a dog is indeed receiving all the nutrients his body needs—and that he isn't consuming too much of any less desirable ingredients. This can also be a great way to offer your dog variety, an element missing from most prepackaged feeding plans. Even if you're feeding your Papillon homecooked foods, introducing just one new healthy food each month can keep both his mind and his mouth wide open.

FEEDING AN OLDER DOG

When your Papillon enters his senior years—at around 9 or 10 years of age—a few more changes in his diet will be necessary. If he has any missing or decaying teeth, that hard kibble that he has been chewing all these years may be better left on the pet supply store shelf. If you worry that your older Papillon has become too set in his ways for a change to an entirely new food, a great alternative is simply pouring some hot water over his dry food to moisten it before serving. Of course, you should always let it cool just a bit to prevent burning your dog's mouth. By softening your dog's food in this way, you can help him enjoy eating again. This slight change in preparation can even help renew an older dog's interest in food if he has become bored with the same bowl of dry kibble day after day. If your Papillon is already eating wet food, try warming it in your microwave for just a few seconds before serving to make it more appealing for him.

Whether you choose to heat things up with plain water or go the canned route, more frequent brushing will be necessary with moist foods. Remember, dental care remains just as important as your dog ages, but you may need to be a bit gentler and more patient in your approach. A dog can still eat surprisingly well with missing teeth, but if you notice any loose or rotten teeth, talk to your veterinarian about having them extracted. If your older dog seems to have lost interest in eating, feeding soft foods alone could solve the problem.

If your dog has developed any health problems with aging, you may also consider placing him on a diet designed to help with his specific issues. This may be as simple as selecting a food containing glucosamine and chondroitin to help ease the aches and pains of arthritis, or asking your veterinarian about diets made for dogs dealing with more serious conditions. Any changes made to your dog's diet should be gradual. If your dog isn't eating the same amount he did in his younger days, consider cutting back on the serving size just a bit. While a decreased appetite is fairly normal for a senior pet, a total loss of appetite is cause for immediate concern. If you can't get your Papillon to eat at all, contact your vet right away.

SPECIAL DIETS AND SUPPLEMENTS

There are two basic categories of specialty foods: those made to maintain the vigor of healthy dogs and supportive diets for sick animals. For example, if your dog has kidney disease, he will need specific foods and lower amounts of protein than other Papillons. Allergy sufferers may require a hypoallergenic diet. Specialty foods for diabetic dogs are also available. High-energy foods for active dogs or organic regimens for dogs of owners with this kind of preference may be purchased at most pet supply stores, but prescription diets designed for dogs suffering or recovering from an illness are only available through licensed veterinarians. Whether your Papillon is fit as a fiddle or he has

Gimmie an A, D, E, B, and K!

Most people know that protein and carbohydrates are excellent sources of energy and that fats help keep a dog's skin and coat in proper condition, but what do vitamins do to keep a dog healthy?

Vitamin:	Vital for:
A	good vision, healthy mucous membranes, strong immune system
D	building strong bones and teeth
E	healthy skin and coat, strong immune system
B	healthy nervous system, efficient metabolism, blood production
K	normal blood clotting

Avoid vitamin C (ascorbic acid, sodium ascorbate, calcium ascorbate, and ascorbyl palmitate) because it can damage your dog's liver and kidneys. If you have trouble remembering which vitamins your Papillon does need, remember the phrase *"A Dog Enjoys Being Kind."*

Discuss your feeding plans with your vet before making any changes to your dog's diet.

hit some stumbling blocks on the road to good health, it is wise to discuss your feeding plans with your vet before making any changes to your dog's diet.

The best way to provide your Papillon with the vitamins and other nutrients his body needs is by serving him healthy food in sensible amounts each day. If your dog suffers from a medical condition, however, your veterinarian may suggest adding certain vitamin supplements to his diet. If your Papillon is healthy, there should be no need to do so unless his diet is lacking something specific. Dogs fed vegetarian diets, for example, may need synthetic taurine, an amino acid naturally found in meat, to maintain good cardiovascular health.

Canine supplements have become amazingly popular in recent years. Your dog's veterinarian may even recommend that you garnish your Papillon's dinner with wheat grass or spirulina, for instance, to help maintain good overall health. While this may be completely harmless, it is important to remember that the word "natural" does not necessarily mean that a particular substance is safe or effective. When given indiscriminately, many natural supplements can even be dangerous to your pet. Interestingly, foods rich in vitamin E have been shown to help fight cancer in human patients, but this healing property appears to be absent when the vitamin is given in supplemental form. To get the green light to offer a specific vitamin or supplement to your dog—and for the proper dosing information for your Papillon's age and weight—always consult your veterinarian.

FEEDING AND EATING PROBLEMS

Eating is one of the greatest pleasures in life, and combining good food with good company can have many positive effects. Studies have shown that children in families that eat together on a regular basis do better in school, get along better with other children, and even eat more nutritious foods. Including your dog in your family's meal times is a great way to expand these great benefits. Dogs are pack animals; they thrive on companionship. So fill your Papillon's bowl and shout out his name whenever you call the rest of your family to breakfast or dinner.

Problems can arise when owners refuse to set proper limits for their pets. Mistakes like overfeeding or allowing a dog to beg for food are serious matters. As adorable as he may be, your Papillon can be a quick study when it comes to learning how to manipulate you, especially if you reward him by giving in to this bad behavior.

Don't Be Pound Foolish!

Being overweight is dangerous for all dogs, but toy breeds face a substantially increased risk of multiple diseases when they carry just a few extra pounds. The line between being just a little too heavy and dangerously obese is never as blurred as it is with Papillons and other dogs of this diminutive size. Conditions like patellar luxation, diabetes, and heart disease are extremely common in these small dogs when they are allowed to gain unnecessary weight. The best way to prevent this from happening is to keep a close eye on your adult dog's weight and adjust his diet and exercise plan accordingly at the slightest fluctuation in that number on the scale.

You can also check your dog's weight by standing him in front of you and gently feeling his chest. His ribs should be discernible but not prominent. If you really have to look for them, your Papillon is probably overweight. Of course, being underweight can be dangerous, too. If your dog's backbone forms an elevated ridge when you move your hand sideways across the middle of his back, this is a sign that he is too thin.

To keep your dog within a healthy weight range, talk to his vet about the best diet for his individual needs. Even if you think you have chosen an ideal food, you could be wrong. High-energy formulas, for example, should only be given to very active dogs—those involved in agility or other highly athletic activities, not those who merely run and play a great deal or go for frequent walks.

Healthy feeding practices combined with daily exercise can keep your dog from becoming overweight.

Obesity

For larger dog breeds, it may take some time before an owner notices an extra pound or two, but on a toy breed just a few pounds can mean the difference between good health and dangerous obesity. In addition to placing your Papillon at a higher risk for many serious illnesses, such as cardiovascular problems and diabetes, extra weight is hard on your dog's joints, making him uncomfortable. It heightens your pet's risk for orthopedic issues like patellar luxation, a knee problem to which this breed is already prone. Just like us, our dogs can gain weight without much effort, but taking it off is usually a far more difficult undertaking. Keeping your pet within a normal weight range is far preferable to allowing him to become overweight or letting those numbers on the scale go up and down repeatedly.

If (like 40 percent of the pets in American homes) your dog is carrying extra weight, you must make his diet and exercise habits your top priorities. An overweight dog may avoid exercising; this can become a vicious cycle because the less a dog moves, the more likely he is to gain more weight. It is also imperative that you begin your Papillon's new exercise plan the same way you would if embarking on a new fitness routine of your own—by seeking the advice of his doctor. Even if your dog is only slightly overweight, you must start out slowly if he is not used to being physically active. Take him for a walk before running around the backyard together, for instance, gradually increasing the pace. This warm-up period can help your pet avoid injuries and even spark his interest for more intense exercise. At first, the walk might be all your dog can handle, but with a strong commitment to this new healthy habit, you will soon see the results in both his appearance and his tolerance for exercise.

Of course, exercise alone will not do the trick. You will also have to decrease the amount of calories your Papillon is consuming in order to decrease his weight. Diet foods can be extremely helpful for this part of the diet plan. If you have become lax in portion control, you may also have to cut back on the amount of food you give your dog. Never eliminate a meal from your dog's routine, and always make sure that he is getting a sufficient amount of nutrition while dieting. Slow and steady wins the race here. It is far healthier for your dog to take weight off slowly. It's all about creating—and sticking to—healthy habits.

Once your dog has reached his goal weight, you can then transition him back to a regular food. You may find that a weight maintenance formula can help keep unwanted pounds off your pet in the future. You must always keep an eye on the amounts and types of all food you give your dog.

Healthy Treats in Moderation

My local pet store has a buffet-style area of every type of dog treat an owner can imagine. Pigs in blankets, bagels, and even yummy cookies are mimicked here in dog-friendly form. Are they cute? Of course. But are they the best snacks for my pets? The answer is found on the label of any product, so always look at the nutritional information before making that impulse purchase. Often the healthier choices are the boxed treats found

Limit the number of treats you offer your dog each day, and make sure they consist only of healthy foods.

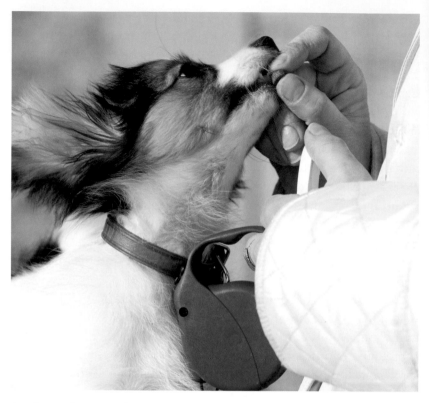

in the aisles near the dog food itself, but even these must be carefully scrutinized.

Just as you would do in choosing a mealtime food for your dog, be selective about the treats you offer him. They should contain no by-products, only healthy preservatives, and low amounts of sugar. You can even buy commercial doggy snacks, like the ones made by Nylabone, that are all-natural and contain no sugar, salt, or preservatives. Treats should also be as low in calories as possible, especially if you plan to offer them regularly.

If you treat your pet with human food, exercise extreme caution. Junk foods like potato chips and cookies (even without those dangerous chocolate chips) are full of empty calories. Instead, opt for healthy snacks like a small amount of fresh fruit and vegetables or tiny cubes of cooked chicken. You don't have to feed excessive amount of fat and calories to indulge your pet. Your Papillon will find a slice of apple just as tasty as a French-fried potato, especially if you never introduce the latter treat as an option.

Finally, limit the number of treats you give your dog each day. The total calories from these impromptu snacks can quickly exceed those in an entire serving of his regular food if you aren't careful. You wouldn't intentionally feed your dog an extra meal each day, right? If you find it difficult to keep track of how many treats you are offering, try setting aside a certain number each day. Once they have been eaten, that's it until tomorrow.

Training Tidbits

Although opinions differ as to whether food should be used as a primary motivator in dog training, many trainers and owners agree that food can be an excellent means of holding your dog's attention while you teach him a specific command or trick—especially if you are having trouble getting your dog to comply with a particular training task. The promise of food just might make the difference between an active canine participant and an easily distracted social butterfly at puppy kindergarten.

With a breed as eager to please as the Papillon, however, food may not be necessary in many training situations. I recommend at least beginning the training process with enthusiastic praise alone. This verbal support from you should be the most important reward your pet receives, and it should always be given, whether you later decide to include edible rewards or not.

If you opt to reward your Papillon with both praise and treats, avoid using the food each time you practice a command. This will help keep his compliance from being dependent on the edible reward. In fact, the history of psychological conditioning states that the best outcomes are achieved when rewards of this kind are given intermittently instead of consistently. Feel free to lavish your dog with as much praise as you like, though. This healthy reward is calorie free!

Even during training, treats should consist of healthy foods. Foods such as dog biscuits are notoriously high in both fat and calories. Also, when training with food, offer tiny treats in moderation, or break biscuits into smaller portions for rewards. Pieces of kibble are great motivators for training, too. As one Papillon breeder put it to me, your dog will work just as hard whether the treat is a tiny crumb or a juicy piece of filet mignon.

Mind Those Manners!

You may not think of table manners as something you need to teach a dog, but if you plan to dine with your Papillon in the

Say Cheese!

If your Papillon puppy's once erect ears are suddenly flopping down, a small change in diet may help. As puppies teethe and grow, their calcium levels fluctuate. Supplementing your dog's kibble regimen with a bit of cottage cheese or plain yogurt (not the sugary stuff) may help get those butterfly-like ears back up in the air. If diet doesn't do the trick, though, rest assured that time will. If your dog had erect ears when you brought him home, they should return to normal soon.

room, you must help him behave properly. The primary reason most dogs misbehave when their owners are eating is that many people frequently give in to their dog's begging. The worst thing you can do if your dog fusses while you eat is share your meal with him. By doing so you are actually teaching him to beg—quite effectively I might add. Once learned, this can be one of the hardest canine habits to break. The key is not giving in to your pet's demands.

Just because you shouldn't feed your Papillon from the table doesn't mean that you should never share food with him. On the contrary, allowing your dog a reasonable portion of a healthy meal—and even serving him his meal alongside the rest of your family—can be an excellent way to show your dog how much you love him. My own dogs would be heartbroken if I were ever to cook corn-on-the-cob without including an extra ear for them. Watching the two of them standing side by side, munching the kernels from the cob as my husband rolls it back and forth for them is one of my favorite summertime joys.

Bad manners arise when a dog begs for food. Your dog may do this by making noise, using his paws to "remind" you of his presence, or simply sitting and staring you in the face while you eat. While some of these behaviors may not bother you too much, they are all begging behaviors that should never be tolerated.

If your dog begs in any way while you are eating, promptly remove him from the table area. Even if the bad behavior occurs near the end of your meal, try to give your pet a chance to rejoin you before you have finished eating. His actions at this point will be a good indication of whether he learned anything from being remanded to his crate or another room. If you are consistent in this approach, he will eventually link the begging to his removal.

When sharing food, prepare your dog's portion at the kitchen counter (instead of placing it in his dish from your plate at the table) to help him understand that his food is his and your food is yours. Also, be sure never to share any food with your dog if he starts begging. Whether the food comes from your plate or the counter, it is imperative that you never reward this behavior.

We all want to give our canine companions the best lives possible, which includes providing optimal nutrition. Although making decisions about how and what to feed your dog may seem daunting at times, the best indication of whether your food choices and feeding schedule are appropriate will be your dog. If he is healthy, active, has a good appetite, and is at a proper weight, then you have fed him successfully.

If your Papillion is healthy, active, and at a proper weight, you've fed him successfully.

5

GROOMING

Your Papillon

The Papillon's trademark hairstyle has an enviable flair, largely due to the dog's beautifully fringed ears. With eye-catching good looks and lively charisma, this darling little pooch possesses the distinctive beauty of a timeless movie star—the Audrey Hepburn of the canine world. While the Papillon may look like a high-maintenance pet, though, it is surprisingly easy to keep everyone who encounters your dog saying "C'est magnifique!"

GROOMING AS A HEALTH CHECK

At first glance, brushing and bathing your dog may seem like aesthetic tasks, but grooming is about so much more than just keeping your Papillon looking good. By taking the time to regularly check his eyes and ears, his teeth and gums, and his coat and nails, you are keeping your finger on the pulse of your dog's health. Countless illnesses have physical signs, but they aren't always apparent unless an owner makes a point of looking for them.

The first thing I always do when preparing to groom my own dogs is massage them thoroughly from head to tail. Over the years I have become quite familiar with their unique body structure, and I know in an instant when something doesn't feel as it should. It was during this preliminary grooming step that I once found a mast cell tumor on one of my dogs—and it was because I located it early that my veterinarian was able to remove it with great success.

The problems you discover won't always be this serious, of course. Perhaps you will notice a strong odor emanating from your dog's ear while rubbing his head—a common symptom of an ear infection. Or, maybe you notice redness in one of your dog's eyes—most likely a sign of conjunctivitis (pink eye). Even these less serious conditions, though, can often alert owners to more menacing problems. In addition to being an irritating affliction of its own, conjunctivitis, for example, can sometimes be a symptom of a more severe illness such as distemper. Most of the time, you won't discover anything out of the ordinary, but knowing what is and isn't normal for your pet is essential to his well-being. And identifying a smaller problem before it can escalate into a larger one is invaluable to your dog's overall health.

BRUSHING

The Papillon is often called a "wash-and-wear" breed, but regular brushing will be necessary whether your dog sports the long, silky hair mentioned in the breed standard or a shorter coat. No matter how plentiful, your dog's single coat will inevitably trap dirt and other debris within it. Brushing removes dead hair and dander. It also helps to keep your dog's fur from shedding all over your clothes and furniture. Because coats can vary so much, there isn't a universal timetable for brushing, but the task should be done at least once a week. Papillons are known for being adept self-groomers, but this is just another reason to grab that brush. You don't want your dog ingesting the remnants of any bacteria or chemicals he has encountered recently.

To prevent hair breakage, always begin brushing by lightly misting your dog's coat with a small amount of water or detangling conditioner. A pin-style brush works best for the Papillon because it is made specifically to reach the skin—the area where most debris settles. Other grooming tools are also useful. Although slicker brushes are too harsh for this breed, you should have a soft-bristled brush for your dog's delicate ears. You also may want to go over mat-prone areas with a fine-toothed comb (literally) once you have finished with the brush. These include behind the Papillon's ears, inside the rear legs,

and the culottes (the long hair on the back of his legs). A comb is an excellent litmus test for thorough brushing. If a snarl still exists, your comb will find it.

There's No Time Like the Present

To help your Papillon accept grooming as a normal part of his routine, begin performing these tasks immediately. Although it may be tempting to allow your new puppy some time to adjust to your household before adding grooming into the equation, don't. A young dog is significantly more receptive to experiences like having his nails trimmed or his teeth brushed than an older dog whose needs have been neglected even for a short period of time. Grooming is not just about aesthetics; it is an important part of your dog's health care routine.

To keep your Papillon looking and feeling his best, brush him once a week.

How to Brush Your Papillon

One of the best ways to avoid hair matting altogether is to use the line-brushing method. Utilized by professional groomers, this technique is surprisingly easy, even for a novice home groomer. Starting at your dog's foot, brush a small layer of hair upwards. This will expose a line of skin and designate a small section of fur. Brush this area thoroughly, first up and then back down. Moving upwards, brush one section of your dog's fur at a time in this way until you have finished the entire leg. Continue this method on your dog's other legs, back, chest, and belly. Beware of brushing upward too intensely, however, because brushing against your dog's hair growth can make your Papillon's fur look puffy, a definite no-no for this breed.

When you find a small section of tangled or matted hair, avoid pulling at it with your brush. Instead, try to separate the hair with your fingers, brushing through just one tiny section at a time. Rubbing a little cornstarch into the mat and letting it work its way into the area for a few minutes before brushing is also said to help make mat removal easier. For larger knots, consider investing in a mat splitter. This sickle-shaped device helps shred the most stubborn mats; however, the remaining fur will usually be more prone to matting as it grows out, so only use this tool as a last resort. The best way to keep your Papillon free of mats and tangles is to brush him every day.

Follow up brushing by removing hair from the pads of your dog's feet. A remarkable number of mats appear in this area, but they are easily overlooked unless an owner is vigilant. Moreover, these dense knots can make walking very uncomfortable for your tiny pet. By keeping this area well trimmed, you can prevent the mats from forming in the first place. Begin by holding your dog's paw while you gently press the center pad to spread the bottom of his foot. This will allow you to reach the excess fur and carefully cut it away with grooming scissors or clippers. (This is also an excellent time to trim your dog's nails.)

BATHING

The most effective way to keep your Papillon clean is to bathe him often, but you may worry that shampooing too frequently will leave your dog's skin dry and itchy. Rest assured that as long as you rinse your dog properly, this should not be a problem—even if you bathe him as often as weekly. On the contrary, regular bathing will stimulate hair growth and prevent breakage.

Preparing for a Bath

The most important step in bathing your Papillon is to brush him beforehand. Bathing a dog with mats will only make them

nearly impossible to remove later. Once you have properly brushed your pet, gather all the things you will need for his bath. This should include a moisturizing shampoo and conditioner, a cup for rinsing (if your sink

For Use in Good Measure

Always check the label to see if your dog's shampoo or conditioner should be diluted before use. Many canine products require this kind of mixing, using a particular ratio of the product to water. Some offer the flexibility of being used either diluted (to various degrees) or in concentrated form. In the former case, you may find it takes some time to find the right mixture for your dog, but you should always begin by using the smallest recommended amount of the product. This will save you money and help to prevent your dog from developing irritated skin from an overly strong solution.

Before bringing your dog to his bath, have all of your supplies set up and ready to go.

or shower does not have a moveable spray nozzle), a washcloth, cotton balls, mineral oil, and at least two large bath towels. Because your Papillon is so small, you may prefer bathing him in your kitchen sink rather than leaning over the bathtub to do the job, but you must use the utmost caution if you do this. A fall from counter height could critically injure or even kill your precious pet. Wherever you choose to draw the bath, use a nonskid mat to prevent him from slipping while standing in the water.

Next, take your dog for a walk to give him a chance to empty his bladder before running his bath water. If you live in a colder climate, this is also the time to turn up your thermostat a bit because your Papillon may feel a bit chilled when he first gets out of the tub. Remember, this may also be the case even in the middle of summer if you use air conditioning. If the day is an especially cold one, postpone bathing until a warmer day.

How to Bathe Your Papillon

Begin the bathing routine by placing a dry cotton ball in each of your dog's ears. After positioning him in the lukewarm water, saturate his coat thoroughly, and using your dampened washcloth, gently wipe his face. This area should not be washed

Before You Buy That Dandruff Shampoo...

Dandruff may be a sign that your dog needs more fat in his diet. If you notice flakes in your Papillon's coat, try adding a small amount of vegetable oil to his food each day. Fish-oil supplements can also be purchased from most veterinarians to help combat dry, itchy skin, and these are typically available in both liquid and capsule forms. Ask your vet if one of these might be right for your pet.

with shampoo because it can irritate your dog's eyes. The washcloth will also come in handy a bit later as you clean your dog's underside and bottom.

Next, dispense a small amount of shampoo into the palm of your hand and work it into a mild lather before applying it to your dog's back. You may notice that canine shampoo doesn't produce the same amount of suds as human shampoo. This is intentional—it makes for easier rinsing. You may also be tempted to spoil your dog by using your own salon brand, but resist this urge. The pH of a dog's skin differs dramatically from a person's, so your high-end products will only leave your Papillon feeling highly uncomfortable. If you truly want to indulge him in spa-style treatment, several designer brands of canine shampoo are available, although you need not spend a fortune for a quality product.

Once you have washed and thoroughly rinsed your pet, follow up by applying a conditioner. Rather than simply rubbing this product over your dog, use your fingers to really work it through the hair. This enables it to reach all his hair and skin. Follow the instructions on the label for the amount of time you should wait before rinsing once again. The great thing about rinsing is that there is no danger of over-doing it, so continue to shower your dog with that H_2O until you are confident that all the shampoo and conditioner has been rinsed down the drain.

Drying After the Bath

To maintain the classic Papillon appearance, follow up by blow drying your dog on a low-heat setting. You may certainly opt to merely towel-dry your pet if the temperature is comfortable, but it may leave his coat looking less than ideal. If you will be showing your dog, using the hairdryer is a must. Even cage dryers, a common tool used by groomers and breeders, are not recommended for use after a preshow bath. The Papillon's coat should be abundant, but not puffy or wavy looking. Brush your dog throughout the drying process. To avoid fluffing the coat too much, brush and dry in the direction of hair growth. Beware of taking your dog outside until his coat is entirely dry, as he may be especially vulnerable to cold air and dirt while he's still damp.

Use special care when blow drying your Papillon's ear fringe.

To maintain the classic Papillon appearance, follow up bathing by blow drying your dog on a low-heat setting.

Position the dryer at the back of your dog's ear as you gently separate and brush the fur with your fingers or a soft-bristled brush. This will help prevent a pointed-ear appearance, a look that is considered a fault in the show ring.

Conversely, at the front of each foot, a bit of hair coming to a point is not only deemed acceptable but desirable. Trimming your dog's coat should only be done when necessary and should be limited to specific areas like the foot, which may need a small amount of scissoring for a neater appearance. Be careful not to trim too much, though, or your Papillon's tootsie might look too much like a cat's paw instead of the hare-like foot described in the breed's standard. Perhaps most importantly, never trim your dog's ears. Just a single ear trim can start an ongoing need for trimming in this area; a natural look is highly preferred.

NAIL TRIMMING

Some people would rather bathe a dog who has had a recent rendezvous with a skunk than trim their nails. I know this because I was once among this well-intended but petrified group of dog owners. Rest assured that if I can overcome my fear of canine pedicures, anyone can. Being able to perform this basic grooming task at home will save you both time and money. It will also increase your confidence for other grooming tasks since this one is by far the most intimidating.

What makes nail trimming so daunting is a little thing called the quick—that sensitive, pink area of the nail (also known as the nailbed) that bleeds if accidentally snipped. The two most important things to know before beginning nail trimming are that first, you will very likely nip your dog's quick at some point in his life, and second, you can stop the bleeding when it does happen. To do so, hold a cold damp cloth on the wound for 10 to 15 minutes, steadily but gently applying pressure. If bleeding persists beyond this point, use styptic powder or a styptic pencil to help speed clotting. Other items that can be used in a pinch are cornstarch, a bar of soap, or a wet tea bag.

Nail trimming is most easily done on a dog who is used to having his feet handled. I recommend gently massaging your dog's feet regularly as soon as you bring him home. This truly is half the battle. If your dog insists on pulling his foot away from you when you hold it, safe trimming is considerably more difficult, not to mention stressful for both you and your pet. So, in the beginning, don't even take the clippers out of your grooming bag.

When to Trim

The rates at which different dogs' nails grow can differ dramatically between individuals, but this task should generally be performed at least once every two to three weeks. As soon as you can hear your dog's nails on the floor, he is already overdue for a trim. Walking on feet with overgrown toenails is painful for

Fuss-Free Grooming

Don't let your Papillon wiggle his way out of being groomed. Even if your dog's constant squirming makes it difficult to finish a particular task in just one session, be tenacious. For example, insist on trimming at least a few nails before putting the clippers away for the day, ending on a positive note whenever possible.

If you give in to fussing or wiggling, you set a dangerous precedent. Although certain grooming tasks can be enjoyable for your pet, remember that grooming is an excellent way to enforce the hierarchy within your home. By making your dog stand for regular grooming, you remind him that you are the one in charge. Even toy breeds need to understand this chain of command. Your persistence can make your dog more accommodating when grooming time arrives again. Praising your Papillon and offering a tasty treat for compliance are also great ways to encourage continued cooperation.

Nail care keeps your dog's feet healthy.

your pet, so don't let this happen. It is better to snip just a tiny bit off his nails more frequently than cut off a longer amount less often. In the former scenario, the quick actually begins to recede in response to the steady trimming, making cutting the quick a much less likely possibility.

Trimming more frequently will also help your dog avoid painful accidents, like snagging his nails in clothing, carpeting, and even his own fur. My dog Jonathan once got one of his nails caught in a neighbor's dog's fur and actually ended up pulling the nail completely out in the process of freeing himself. At the time, he was only slightly overdue for a pedicure. Could a more recent trim have prevented this dreadful mishap? I can't say for certain, but I believe it likely may have.

How to Trim Your Papillon's Nails

The easiest way to trim your Papillon's nails is by placing him in standing position. Holding the foot, gently press on your dog's paw pad to extend the toenail. Using your clippers, snip off just the hook-like end of the nail on a 45-degree angle. Remember, taking too little is better than cutting too much.

Ear Infection Caution

Ear infections rarely affect both of a dog's ears. When they do, they are almost always caused by cross-contamination during cleaning. To prevent this from happening, always use a fresh cotton ball for each ear.

Always err on the side of caution. Repeat this process on all your dog's nails, including dew claws if present. I like to finish each session by walking my dogs on a coarse surface such as pavement or concrete, which helps smooth any rough edges on the nails. You may also use an emery board for this purpose.

Some dog owners prefer using a nail grinder to trim their pets' nails. This hand-held rotary tool works like a high-speed emery board. If you think this device may work well for you, ask your dog's veterinarian to show you how to use it properly before trying it out on your Papillon. Although any wounds that might result from a grinder will be instantly cauterized, they can still hurt. Also, be careful not to allow any fur to wrap around the spinning rotary bit.

Although accidents may happen from time to time, be sure you aren't cutting your Papillon's quick too frequently. If you are, consider deferring the task to a professional groomer or your dog's veterinarian. This is preferable to injuring your pet on a regular basis. Your dog will forgive an occasional accident, but frequent mishaps could cause him to fear nail trimming and could even lead to a dangerous infection.

EAR CARE

Although Papillons are not among the breeds most susceptible to ear infections, routine cleaning is the best way to ensure that your dog won't suffer from this uncomfortable condition. An ideal time to clean your dog's ears is either right before or immediately after his bath, but this should not be the only time you perform this important task. Ideally, you should clean your dog's ears at least once a week.

Begin by sniffing the ear. It shouldn't smell foul in any way. If you notice a strong odor, contact your veterinarian because this is a sign of infection. Other red flags include redness, discharge, or sensitivity to touch. Abstain from cleaning the ear if your dog shows any of these symptoms. Not only can cleaning be painful for a pet suffering from an ear infection, but it can also make it difficult for a vet to accurately diagnose the problem.

How to Groom Your Papillon's Ears

Canine ear cleansers are widely available, but try to avoid those containing alcohol and hydrogen peroxide because they can irritate sensitive skin. A great natural alternative is mixing your own cleaning solution of equal parts vinegar and water. Using a squeezable bottle, squirt a small amount of the solution into your dog's ear canal. He will likely respond to this by shaking his head. Although he may get you a little wet, this is actually a good thing because this vigorous movement only helps to spread the cleanser and loosen dirt and other debris within the ear. You can also rub the ear from the outside to help with this process.

Once your Papillon has finished flailing about, use a cotton ball (never a swab) to gently wipe the inside of his ear. If the ear is especially dirty, you will notice a dark coloration on the cotton. Continue wiping the ear with fresh cotton balls until they come out mostly clean. Remember, a small amount of wax is necessary, so the cotton doesn't have to look pristine. Repeat this process on the second ear.

EYE CARE

Taking care of your dog's eyes is probably the easiest of all grooming tasks. All you must do is keep them clean, make a point of checking them regularly for any signs of a problem, and seek veterinary treatment if a problem is discovered. Look for symptoms such as redness, discharge, and cloudiness.

Aah, This Is the Life!

When I indulge in a long bath or pedicure, I feel relaxed and rejuvenated, certainly not stressed. Wouldn't it be wonderful if pets felt pampered during grooming activities like we humans do? They can! Begin each grooming session by gently massaging your Papillon. As you brush him, tell him how handsome he is in your most soothing voice. Or, end nail trimming with a brisk walk around the neighborhood. In addition to providing your pet with a fun reward, this will also help smooth any jagged edges on his nails.

How you choose to indulge your dog matters much less than taking the time to do it. By going this extra mile, you can transform grooming from a series of mundane tasks to special bonding time you spend with your pet.

To keep your dog's eyes clean, gently wipe them daily with a soft, wet cloth.

Although tear staining is common in many light-colored dogs, it can sometimes indicate a problem such as a clogged or infected tear duct. Injuries can also cause eye problems, so take care when walking your dog outdoors or placing new furniture in your home.

How to Groom Your Papillon's Eyes

Keeping the eyes clean is a simple task. All you need to do is gently wipe them daily with a soft cloth dipped in distilled water. This will help keep them free of debris and even prevent normal tear staining. I have found that using an artificial tear solution daily also significantly reduces my own dog's eye discharge.

A great preventive measure for heading off many eye problems is having your Papillon's peepers checked regularly by a canine ophthalmologist. Your dog's vet may be able to recommend a doctor, or you can contact the American College of Veterinary Ophthalmologists at www.acvo.org for the name of an ophthalmologist in your area. Unlike your regular veterinarian, an eye doctor won't need to see your Papillon annually, but routine exams every few years will help identify any emerging problems.

DENTAL CARE

Keeping your Papillon's teeth and gums clean and healthy will make life more pleasant for both you and your pet. Even small amounts of plaque and tartar can leave an otherwise delightful little dog with breath that could knock over a Great Dane. Additionally, good dental hygiene helps maintain good overall health. When your dog swallows bacteria, it is transported throughout his body. These harmful microorganisms can leave your Papillon vulnerable to countless medical conditions, including heart and kidney disease. Neglecting dental care will also inevitably lead to tooth decay, and likely tooth loss, as your pet ages.

Good canine dental care begins with what you choose to feed your dog. Because kibble is dry, it won't calcify on your dog's teeth as quickly as canned or homecooked foods. If you do feed your Papillon soft or wet foods, be sure to give him plenty of crunchy treats such as raw carrots and other vegetables. Many dental-friendly treats available at most pet supply stores, such as the ones made by Nylabone, are made specifically to reduce plaque and tartar buildup. Regular brushing will be necessary, though, no matter what your dog eats.

Banishing Doggy Breath

One of the least talked about but most commonly treasured parts of owning a dog is "puppy breath." Many dog lovers compare this unique smell to that of a new car. It is instantly identifiable, albeit somewhat of an acquired taste, and sadly (at least to those who adore it) it only lasts a short time. This perfectly normal and healthy scent is in part the result of a dog's early diet—mother's milk, puppy food, and the enzymes that break down these nutrients. It is also frequently due to gas escaping from a puppy's stomach through his immature esophagus. Older puppies may even experience a second surge of stinky breath when they begin losing their baby teeth. This typically only lasts as long as it takes the adult teeth to grow into place, though.

True bad breath, on the other hand, is a matter for concern. Caused by tartar and gum disease, worms, or coprophagia (eating feces), this problem isn't only unpleasant for those who share a dog's air space, but it is also a serious issue that should never be overlooked. Left ignored, it can lead to a number of dangerous health issues, including kidney and liver failure. The best way to avoid those repercussions is by brushing your dog's teeth as often as possible. You should also bring stool samples whenever you take your dog for a routine exam so that your vet can check for the presence of worms. If you suspect your dog is eating his own feces, try adding a small amount of meat tenderizer or acidophilus to his dog food.

Occasionally, a dog can suffer from a temporary case of bad breath due to a specific food item he has ingested. To help keep your Papillon's breath smelling sweet, add some liquid chlorophyll to his water dish or garnish his dinner bowl with a bit of chopped mint or parsley—and follow up by brushing his teeth. Because charcoal absorbs toxins and works as a natural purifier, biscuits containing this ingredient may also help alleviate a mild case of canine halitosis. (Incidentally, charcoal biscuits are great for upset tummies, too!) If bad breath is indeed a warning sign of a health issue, though, it will persist. This is the time to contact your dog's veterinarian to rule out a more serious cause.

Inspect and clean your dog's teeth as part of his regular grooming routine.

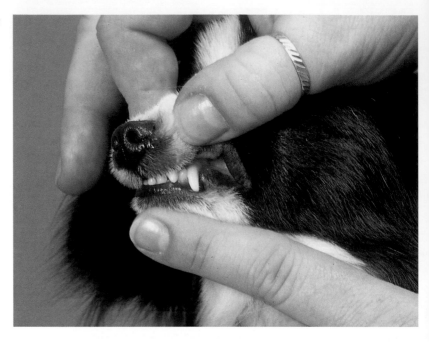

How to Brush Your Papillon's Teeth

Because the Papillon's mouth is so tiny, you may opt to use a simple piece of sterile gauze in lieu of a toothbrush. Another great alternative is a finger brush, a soft plastic brush that fits over the tip of your finger and easily into the mouths of even toy dogs. Even larger dogs often balk at the prospect of allowing a standard-sized canine toothbrush into their mouths.

Whether your dog tolerates his toothbrush well or not, one thing he will almost certainly like is the toothpaste itself. Unlike human toothpaste, canine toothpaste comes in a wide variety of dog-friendly flavors, such as beef, poultry, and seafood. The enticing tastes and smells may even be enough to make your dog enjoy having his pearly whites cleaned. Baking-soda and tartar-control formulas are also available. Never use your own toothpaste on your pet, though, because it can make him sick.

Begin by offering your dog a small amount of his toothpaste on your bare finger. As soon as he realizes that it tastes as good as it smells, he will be more open to the brushing process. Using a circular motion, begin brushing just one tooth at a time, concentrating on the area where the tooth meets the gum line. This is the spot where tartar tends to accumulate. If your dog is particularly resistant, try spreading the task out over a few days, ending on a positive note whenever possible. As you gradually increase the number of teeth you clean at each sitting, you should be able to perform at least two to three complete brushing sessions a week. Daily brushings are even better! Although rinsing isn't necessary, I like to follow up brushing my dogs' teeth by giving them a cool drink of water and taking them for their morning walk. This helps integrate the task into our daily routine.

When a dog owner doesn't make dental care a priority, professional cleanings and tooth extractions usually become necessary. This process requires general anesthesia, which is best avoided whenever possible for all pets, but especially for the Papillon, who is extremely vulnerable to the dangers of anesthetics. Regular tooth brushing is highly preferable to this risky option.

Most importantly, if you aren't able to brush your dog's teeth every day, don't give up. This is not an all-or-nothing task. Brushing just twice a month is better than not at all.

6

TRAINING *and* BEHAVIOR
of Your Papillon

Ask three different dog owners what expectations they have for their pets and you will likely receive three very different answers. One owner might not allow dogs on the furniture, while another may enjoy sharing her bed pillow with her Papillon every night. Yet another might not have a strong opinion about which (if any) pieces of furniture are off limits, but might find it completely unacceptable for his Papillon to jump up on people. While there are very few hard and fast rules dictating what your dog should and shouldn't be allowed to do, one thing is certain: If you don't train your Papillon, he will surely train himself.

Many owners of toy breeds mistakenly assume that teaching their dogs what is and isn't acceptable in their homes is somehow less important because of their pets' diminutive size. I assure you that a 10-pound Papillon is no less capable of destroying an expensive pair of shoes or soiling your wall-to-wall carpeting than a full-grown Dalmatian or Doberman Pinscher. Though he may not be quite as loud as one of these larger breeds, your Papillon is also just as likely to annoy you and anyone else within earshot if he is allowed to bark excessively. Whatever your rules, you must establish them early and stick to them. If a regression occurs, you must act promptly. Little dogs learn bad behaviors as quickly as any other breed.

TRAINING BEGINS AT HOME

You may not even realize it at the time, but you will begin training your Papillon the minute you bring him home. Dogs are always learning from their surroundings. Whether you focus your efforts on actively teaching your pet obedience commands or you train him instead by tolerating problem behaviors, he will repeat any action for which he receives a reward. Bear in mind that reinforcement comes in many forms. An edible treat or praise may be the most effective of these, but don't discount the impact of allowing a particular behavior to become a habit. When your

Positive training is important for any dog—even a small one. It will help him fit into your family routine and enable him to feel secure because he will know what is expected of him.

dog is permitted to keep one of your personal belongings simply because he has already chewed it beyond its usefulness, for instance, what he learns is that destructive chewing is a means of shopping for new toys.

Believe it or not, simple tasks such as attaching your dog's leash whenever you venture outdoors or making your Papillon walk to his elimination spot instead of carrying him there are important training tasks. When viewed this way, the broader job of training can be broken down into smaller, more manageable steps. Training is not something you merely fit into your weekly schedule; it encompasses everything you do with your pet on a daily basis.

SETTING CLEAR TRAINING GOALS

A well-trained dog is not only a blessing to his family, but he is also a welcome guest practically anywhere his owner takes him. Even if you never plan to enter your dog in a formal obedience trial, this doesn't mean he won't benefit from learning simple commands such as sitting or staying. Whatever your training goals, consider them carefully before planning your training schedule.

Perhaps you simply want a well-behaved companion. If this is the case, you may be able to learn everything you need to know by attending puppy kindergarten or reading about basic obedience and teaching your pet the commands you learn. If you plan to show your Papillon in conformation, it will be especially helpful for him to continue past introductory training or to receive instruction from a professional trainer. If you have a clear idea of what you want to train for, it will make the task much easier.

HOW TO FIND A PROFESSIONAL TRAINER

The concept of sending a dog to a trainer always struck me as an undermining practice. Sure, the dog may learn a variety of commands and might even be able to demonstrate them initially upon returning home, but will he respond to you as well as the person who trained him? Certainly a trainer has a valuable role in the process of teaching our dogs what we want them to do, but that role should focus more on teaching us how to effectively train our dogs on an ongoing basis at home.

Nowadays, trainers can be found virtually everywhere: through business cards posted at your local pet supply store, in your phone book's Yellow Pages, and even online. Selecting the right one, however, requires a bit more effort. With so many different training methods available, you should start with the style of training that you desire (leash and collar, reward-based, clicker training, etc.). Next, ask for referrals from your veterinarian or local animal shelter because these resources will lead you to the most reputable trainers in your area. You may also contact the Association of Pet Dog Trainers at (800) PET-DOGS or www.apdt.com for the name of a trainer near you. Knowledge of canine health and behavior, as well as experience with toy breeds specifically, is certainly a plus.

Ask if you can sit in on a training class before enrolling your Papillon. While there, watch the people and their pets. Do they seem to be enjoying themselves? Is there an open line for communication between the trainer and the pet owners? The answers to both these questions should be an obvious yes. Are

Practice Makes Perfect

Although attending a dog training class is a great way to learn how to train your Papillon, this group setting shouldn't be the only time and place you work on training with your pet. Practice is essential for reinforcing the commands you begin teaching your dog in class. With the constant distraction of the other owners and their dogs, your Papillon may not perform the desired behaviors even while there. Classes are primarily for teaching owners how to train their pets. Even if you and your puppy do your homework faithfully after each lesson, you must continue to make training a priority once the class concludes. It takes a lot longer than six weeks to effectively train a dog.

multiple family members encouraged to attend classes? While space is sometimes limited, being able to include all members of your household in your dog's training is a definite advantage.

Health precautions should rank among a trainer's top priorities. For this reason, certain vaccinations may be prerequisites to admission into the class. While these safety measures are intended to protect your pet, you must always discuss the pros and cons of vaccination with your Papillon's veterinarian. If you are uncomfortable with a specific shot a class requires, it may be better to hire a trainer who will come to you instead of bringing your dog to a group setting.

Training should always be positive. Avoid trainers who use choke collars or electronic aids such as shock collars. Likewise, anyone who yells at an animal is bad news. Listen to your instincts, and also watch your dog's reactions to different individuals. If he dislikes or fears a particular person, keep looking. Dogs are among the best judges of human character.

Even if your training goals are modest, I highly recommend bringing your Papillon puppy to a beginner's training class. This weekly or bi-weekly outing offers your pet the opportunity to socialize with other dogs and their owners, as well as receive the obvious benefit of learning basic obedience commands at an early age. Having a network of fellow dog owners can also be extremely helpful for you. The trainers will teach you how to train your pet, but the new friends you find can commiserate with you over any challenges you face and join you in celebrating your dog's accomplishments.

INVOLVING THE WHOLE FAMILY IN TRAINING

In addition to encouraging family members to attend training classes with you and your pet, ask for their help in putting your new knowledge into practice. If you are the only one who walks your dog or feeds him, he may depend on you too intensely—or worse, behave badly for others when they must care for him. Most importantly, the other people living in your dog's household mustn't work against your training efforts. If you want your dog to sit before receiving his dinner each night, and your husband simply puts your dog's dish before him, your dog will receive mixed messages.

If you have children, they too play an important part in properly training your dog. Believe it or not, the younger your kids are, the more important it is that you include them in this process. Certainly, you cannot trust your preschooler to hold your dog's leash while teaching him to heel, but you can ask her to help you praise your pet when he sits. Never trust a small child alone with any animal (or vice versa), but teaching your child to properly care for and respect an animal will help safeguard them both from potential rivalry issues. You will also be exposing your children to one of the most rewarding parts of life—the loving relationships that result from the humane treatment of animals.

One of the greatest advantages of involving the entire family in the training process is that it enables you to match the best person to each task. Perhaps you easily taught your Papillon to sit and stay, but you lack the precise timing necessary to successfully teach the enough command for interrupting barking. If so, another family member may have better luck. Even if you are stressed or simply in a poor mood, it may be preferable to have your spouse or older child assume the dog training tasks for a while. Dogs are incredibly empathic beings; our fluctuating human moods often affect them deeply, and this can, in turn, affect their training progress.

REWARD-BASED TRAINING

One of the best and most positive ways to train your Papillon is to use food and praise as rewards when he exhibits a desired behavior. Many trainers use this type of reward-based training because it reinforces positive behaviors and avoids using

Consistency Rules!

Should your puppy sleep in bed with you or in his crate? Will he go outside for housetraining, or will he use an indoor littor box? The answers to these questions may vary from one Papillon owner to another, but one thing should always remain the same: consistency. Whatever rules you establish, you must set them early and stick to them if you expect your dog to learn them. Also, be sure to let other household members know your rules. If you don't allow your Papillon on the sofa but your children do, your dog will receive mixed messages. Be consistent, and he will quickly learn what you expect of him.

punishment as a motivator to behave appropriately. Some dogs respond to praise, but most owners find that food is a universal primary motivator when it comes to canines.

To apply this method of training, use a positive tone of voice to praise your Papillon as soon as he performs a particular command, while simultaneously offering a treat. Timing is crucial with this kind of training, so it can be helpful to have a professional trainer show you the ropes. Also, the treats used as rewards should be extremely tiny so that your Papillon doesn't fill up too quickly during training sessions. Treats can consist of anything your dog finds tasty—cut up pieces of hot dog, cheese, chicken, etc.

As your dog begins to show some success, continue to offer praise each time a task is performed, but offer the food reward more sporadically. Food rewards should be gradually phased out as new tasks are mastered. You may want to return to food rewards, however, whenever you introduce a new command.

The more verbal praise you offer along with rewards, the easier time you will have eliminating the food. Never cease to praise your dog when he follows your commands. Although treats help to hold your dog's attention and reinforce success, his biggest reward is seeing that his master is pleased with a job well done.

Always train your dog before he has eaten: he will be more interested in earning the reward, and you will be able to adjust the portion of his next meal accordingly. If your dog is no longer a puppy and is already carrying some extra weight, be especially vigilant. Generally, dogs who respond best to food rewards are those who aren't overfed at other times.

HOUSETRAINING

Toy breeds have a reputation for being difficult to housetrain, but the truth is that housetraining success depends more on the owner than the dog. The more consistent you are in your approach, the more quickly your Papillon will become reliably trained. Giving your new pet some time to adjust to his household before beginning housetraining, however, will inevitably delay this process. The key is establishing a schedule as soon as your dog arrives home—and then sticking to it.

Know the Signs

Because they have tiny bladders, toy breeds need to be taken out more frequently. Make sure you can recognize all the signs that your Papillon needs to eliminate. Most dogs have pre-elimination gestures; some walk in circles, others sniff the ground. Your dog may do something entirely unique to him. Once you have a better idea of what these telltale signs are, you can reinforce housetraining and also help prevent accidents.

When housetraining your dog, choose a spot in your yard where you want him to eliminate and take him to that designated area every time.

Without a schedule, even a fully trained pet can regress. For this important reason, even an adopted dog who has been previously housetrained should be treated as though he is untrained during the first few weeks he acclimates to his new home.

Introducing Housetraining

The first step in successful housetraining is selecting the place where your pet will eliminate. Most dog owners take their pets outside to do their business, but some Papillon owners prefer to paper train their pets or provide them with litter boxes. Because these tiny dogs similarly have smaller bladders, offering them an indoor bathroom makes it possible for them to eliminate at any time of day, whether their owners are home or not. Conversely, indoor elimination requires an increased amount of cleanup. Owners who prefer not to clean a litter box may opt for outdoor training for this reason. Whichever spot you choose, take your dog there—and only there—for elimination until he becomes trained. Walking your dog in different areas or moving his papers from one area of your home to another will only confuse him.

Toy breeds may do well with paper training or a litterbox.

Toy breeds may do well with paper training or a litterbox.

Paper Training

If you go the paper-training route, begin by spreading several layers of newspaper across a large section of the floor in the room where your Papillon will eliminate. Whenever your puppy urinates or defecates on the paper, praise him immediately. Punishing your dog when he misses the paper, though, will only confuse him. Dogs live in the moment. Both praise and reprimands are fruitless if delivered at the wrong moment. Punishment in any form will be much more likely to damage your relationship with your Papillon than help him to understand what he has done wrong.

The best thing to do when your dog has an accident is ignore it. Postpone picking up the mess until you have removed your dog from the scene because watching you may leave him with the mistaken notion that it's his job to make the messes and yours to clean them up. A crate can be very helpful at these times, but a baby gate also works well to safely contain your Papillon during cleanup times.

As your dog begins catching on, progressively make the paper-covered section of your floor smaller and smaller until it only takes up a portion of the original space. In the beginning, remove only a layer or two of the soiled paper; doing so will help remind your puppy where he should go the next time the urge strikes. Be sure to remove those top layers, though, as a dirty potty spot can actually discourage a pet from going where he should. No one likes to use a dirty bathroom. Once your dog is consistently going on his papers, remove all the affected papers to keep the area as clean as possible.

Outdoor Housetraining

If you take your dog to your backyard to eliminate, you can still utilize his acute sense of smell to help remind him where he should go. Even when you clean an outdoor area by hosing it with water, your dog will still be able to detect the scent of urine left behind. Additionally, for the first week or two of training, leave his last bowel movement on the grass until the next time he defecates. If your Papillon eliminates indoors, move the stool to the yard where he is supposed to go, or take the wet paper towel used to clean the puddle of urine to this same location. Although it seems rather literal, this is the best way to show your pet the right place for elimination.

Potty Schedules

Whether you choose to paper train your Papillon or take him outdoors for elimination, keep an eye on the clock and bring him to your chosen area at least every two hours when your puppy is eight weeks old. With each additional month of age, the time period he should be able to wait between trips will increase by another hour, with a maximum limit of approximately six hours. At first, this will mean making about 10 to 12 elimination trips each day, but take heart—by the time your dog is just 6 months old, he should only be heading to his potty spot between 4 and 6 times daily as he becomes reliably housetrained.

If your dog doesn't eliminate within the first few minutes at his potty spot, leave the area together. Keep a close eye on him while you wait about 20 minutes before making a return trip. He will go eventually, but you must be patient. Your job as his owner is to increase the odds that he goes in the right spot when that time comes.

Move Training to the Next Level

Once your dog is consistently performing your commands more than 85 percent of the time, start training in a variety of new places. If you only practice commands at home, your Papillon may only respond to your instructions while in this one area. Once he learns to comply in other environments, he will become equally dependable at home and in more hectic or unfamiliar surroundings.

Avoid saying, "Go potty!" or whatever other words you want your pet to associate with elimination. Your Papillon may or may not learn to eliminate on command, but using these words before your dog does his duty will only decrease the odds that he links the words to the correct behavior. Instead, utter your chosen phrase as soon as your dog begins to eliminate. Most dogs have pre-elimination gestures, but these can be different for each animal. Some walk in circles; others sniff the ground. Your dog may do something entirely unique to him. Watch for his signs, and you will have a better idea of when to give it another few minutes and when to head back inside. Knowing your dog's telltale signs can also help you prevent accidents.

Unfortunately, accidents are an inevitable part of the housetraining process, but you can help keep them from recurring by thoroughly cleaning any soiled areas. The same strong sense of smell that helps remind your dog of the right place to eliminate can also prompt him to eliminate once again in the spot of a previous accident. A product made specifically for cleaning up after pets is essential, as is keeping a full roll of paper towels handy at all times. No cleaning product can remove the odor of urine if you don't completely absorb the wetness.

Housetraining Tools

A dog may be taught to let his owner know when he needs to relieve himself. A great tool for this purpose is a bell. A strip of holiday jingle bells or even a cow bell will do the job nicely. Simply hang the item on or beside your door and help your dog

Middle-of-the-Night Potty Trips

Most young puppies cannot go all night without getting up to relieve themselves at least once. The best way to limit this is by making sure your dog has a bowel movement after his dinner and offering him no food after this time. Your Papillon's water bowl should be removed at least two hours before bedtime, and he should be taken for one last opportunity to eliminate before calling it a night. Even when these preemptive steps are taken, though, your puppy may still need a middle-of-the-night potty break during those first few weeks at home.

A good sign that your dog needs to eliminate is if he becomes restless during the night. The second you wake to find your dog wandering, jump up to take him to his potty spot as quickly as possible. Picking him up and holding him while you find your shoes and coat is a great way to interrupt him. An even more certain sign that your dog needs this extra trip outdoors is if you are waking up to discover that accidents have taken place. Rest assured that these midnight treks to the backyard won't last forever. Before you know it, your little puppy will be several months old and fully housetrained, and you will be sleeping like a baby.

touch it each time you open the door to head to his potty spot. To prevent him from getting his toenails caught, encourage him to use his nose instead of his paws to touch this noisemaker. Your dog will quickly begin to relate the sound this object makes with going outdoors. To discourage him from using the bell to ask for walks, however, use it only when you take him out to do his business.

Having a new puppy in the house can sometimes be an overwhelming experience. You may forget the exact time of your Papillon's last feeding or when the last housetraining accident occurred. For this reason, I recommend using a chart. As elementary as it might seem, this is the best way to keep track of when you dog eats, drinks, and eliminates during those early weeks. It can also give you a clear picture of his progress. As a general rule, your dog should need to void his bladder and bowels shortly after each meal. He will also need to urinate whenever he wakes from a nap or you finish a vigorous play session.

Transitional Housetraining Methods

While you shouldn't expect your Papillon to repeatedly toggle between indoor and outdoor housetraining, some situations warrant a transition. Perhaps you will move to an apartment building where the policy states that all dogs need to eliminate outdoors. Or maybe your older dog can no longer manage the cold as well as he did when he was younger. In some cases, illness (either your own or your dog's) makes a transition to indoor elimination necessary. Whatever the circumstances, a transition is possible, but it will likely take both time and effort.

In some cases, owners prefer to begin housetraining indoors and then move toward outdoor elimination as their puppy attains some success with paper training. The theory here is that younger dogs will likely be more adaptable to making the transition. While this may indeed be true, it is still less than an ideal way to teach a puppy your expectations. If you are certain from the beginning that you want your Papillon to eliminate outdoors, it is far better to begin using this method of training from the start.

If you're certain you want your Papillon to eliminate outdoors, it's best to use this method of housetraining from the start.

Transitioning to Outdoor Elimination

If you need to train your indoor dog to relieve himself outdoors, the best way to start is by bringing the indoor potty out with you. Whether your Papillon uses a litter box or newspapers, taking either item outdoors will help show him that the rules are changing.

Before starting the transition, take note of your dog's schedule of indoor elimination and begin taking him outdoors at those same times. As with your original training, praise your dog effusively whenever he goes potty outdoors. Eventually, you will be able to do away with the litter box (or newspapers), but wait until your dog has mastered the task of using it in its new location before doing so.

Transitioning to Indoor Paper Training

Transitioning a dog from outdoor elimination to using papers or a little box may prove a bit more difficult than the other way around, but it is possible if an owner is patient and plans ahead. Begin by bringing a small part of the new method outside with you when your dog goes out to relieve himself. Place a newspaper or a handful of litter on your dog's regular potty spot immediately upon reaching his outdoor potty spot. Encourage your dog to go as you normally would, but on the new item. As with all forms of training, praise your Papillon immensely when he does as you ask.

Once your dog has achieved some success with going on the paper or litter outdoors, introduce the litter box by placing it outside beside the outdoor potty area, and then begin encouraging him to go inside the box. As he becomes more and more comfortable with using the indoor paraphernalia, start gradually moving the papers or box away from the outdoor spot and closer to your home. The ultimate challenge will be moving the items indoors, where you will still continue instructing your dog where the appropriate potty spot is whenever it is time for elimination.

CRATE TRAINING

Housetraining can certainly be made easier by incorporating crate training into your Papillon puppy's routine. Because dogs prefer not to soil themselves, a crate quickly becomes an off-limits area for accidents. This provides you with an ideal location for your pet when you cannot properly supervise him during housetraining. Be sure your dog's crate isn't too big, though, or you may find him using one end as a bedroom and the other as a bathroom. Also, only keep your dog in his crate for reasonable amounts of time. Even a fully trained adult dog should never be left in his crate for more than the six-hour maximum between trips for elimination.

During housetraining in the crate, remove your Papillon's water bowl an hour or two before bedtime to prevent middle-of-the-night accidents, but whenever you leave your dog in his crate at other times, it is extremely important to always

There Is a Reason They Call It Crate *Training*

You mustn't expect your Papillon to embrace his crate the very first time you use it. Although it shouldn't be extremely taxing, crate training takes time. Likewise, you cannot use the crate only sporadically if you want your dog to accept it as a regular part of his routine.

When used correctly, the crate can be an effective means of keeping your Papillon safe and for providing him with a special space of his own. If you only take it out when traveling or when an unfamiliar person enters your home, your Papillon will be unlikely to ever feel truly comfortable in it.

provide him with fresh drinking water. If you find that the plastic dishes that came with your dog's crate are too small or prone to spilling, consider replacing them with either stainless steel versions or a water bottle. Smaller dogs can easily be taught to drink from these convenient containers, which attach to the outside of the crate door.

Crate Training Benefits

Crate training offers many benefits to pet owners and dogs alike. The crate, or kennel, is a wonderful place for your pet to take naps or enjoy a bone or edible treat. You may even find your dog heading to his crate without any prompting at various times throughout the day. If you want your dog to view his kennel as a place of refuge, though, you must never use it for punishment. Even when you escort your dog to his crate after a housetraining accident so you can clean the mess, avoid using a harsh tone.

Crating is also a wonderful means of protecting your Papillon from people who may unintentionally do him harm. Certainly, no one you invite to your home would mean to hurt your precious pet, but toy breeds have a way of getting underfoot during parties and other gatherings with numerous guests. Your dog may also be safer in his crate when your guests bring extremely young children or pets whose temperaments are unreliable.

Introducing the Crate

At first, your goal should be to merely introduce the crate to your Papillon. Leave the door open, and place a treat inside the kennel to make it more inviting. When your puppy enters the

Training Older Papillons

When it comes to learning, puppies are virtually blank canvases. Because they have not had the time to accumulate many bad habits, their owners can spend training time introducing fun new tasks instead of holding remedial lessons. Young dogs are often extremely quick to repeat desired behaviors. Owners of older pets, however, often face more challenges in the training department. Perhaps your adopted Papillon was never fully housetrained, or maybe he was allowed to chew on inappropriate items. Your more mature pet is just as capable of correcting these behaviors—and learning those proverbial new tricks—as a younger dog. He may just need a little extra time and patience to achieve the same level of success. The pride he feels from his accomplishments, though, will be instantaneous, so be sure to celebrate his successes whether you've been working on a particular command for a single afternoon or for the last few weeks.

If you want your dog to be comfortable in his crate, you must use it consistently.

crate, praise him. Avoid shutting the door until he is entering the crate on a regular basis, and even then only close it for short periods of time. Try to end each training exercise on a positive note. If your dog resists being crated, wait until he stops fussing (even if this is a period of just a few quiet seconds) before opening the door.

As your dog adjusts to spending time inside his crate with the door closed, move on to leaving the room after you place him in it, gradually lengthening the duration. Again, always praise him for his good behavior. If your dog starts off doing well but begins fussing toward the end of the confinement period, consider this a sign that you are moving too fast. You still must not let him out of the crate when he cries, though. If you do, he quickly will learn that all he has to do to get out is make some noise. Remember, dogs are always learning!

Reinforcing Crate Time

If you want your dog to be comfortable in his crate, you must use it consistently. Even if your Papillon acclimates to using a crate or kennel early, he could have trouble readjusting to it if he is only inside of it a few times a year. Many people are tempted to skip crating once a dog is reliably housetrained, but this can force owners and their pets to repeat the entire crate-training process. If you would like to offer your Papillon free run of the family home, alternate between doing so and using the crate. This ensures that he will readily head to his crate whenever he must spend some time there.

Crating for Travel

If you plan to travel with your pet, crating will be virtually unavoidable. Whether you fly or drive, a crate is the safest place for your pet during transport. Even if you use a boarding service when you take vacations or go on business trips, your Papillon will likely still need to spend some time in a structure of this kind. Making him as comfortable as possible with the crating concept will help ease any anxiety he feels about traveling or being away from you during these times.

If your Papillon came from a puppy mill, though, you may never be able to create a positive association to a crate. Dogs bred in these large-scale facilities are kept in crates for most of their young lives and forced to eat and sleep in their own excrement. Not only will a puppy mill dog fear the crate due to this horrible history, but he will also be much more likely to eliminate inside of it because this is what he had to do for the weeks before arriving in your home. In this situation, a well-placed baby gate is highly preferable to a crate.

LEASH TRAINING

I would be willing to bet that very few people bringing Rottweiler puppies home forget to buy leashes before homecoming day. Owners of toy breeds, though, may think this item is somehow less necessary. They are so wrong! Walking on leash is something that every dog—regardless of size—must learn. Even if you have a fenced yard in which your dog spends most of his outdoor time, there will inevitably be occasions when he must walk in public.

Leash Training Benefits

It is certainly easy to carry a toy breed in your arms, but you

Aside from keeping your dog safe, walking on leash makes socializing your pet much easier.

will be doing your Papillon a great disservice if you never allow him to walk on the ground. Walking on leash helps give your dog a sense of adventure, and it makes socializing your pet much easier. When held in their owners' arms, many dogs focus more on protecting their masters than on meeting and greeting new friends.

Introducing Leash Training

Attach your puppy's leash to his collar multiple times throughout each day, starting the day you bring him home. If you wait until he is older, he may be fearful of the leash when you finally use it. This simple tether could possibly save your dog's life one day. I recommend using a leash even when you plan to carry your pet for this reason. It only takes a second for your Papillon to jump off your lap and bolt into a dangerous situation. To further ensure his safety, always supervise your dog when he is wearing his leash because it may get caught on something and injure or choke him.

Start venturing outside with your new pet for walks immediately. Many dogs acclimate quickly to walking on leash when the task is introduced early, but occasionally even a young walker will start pulling you excitedly in this direction and that. If your Papillon pulls, stop walking at once. This will interrupt his pulling and show him that doing this behavior won't get him anywhere—literally. Be sure to pay close attention because the gentle pulling of this breed may easily be overlooked, but it should never be tolerated.

BASIC OBEDIENCE

Teaching your Papillon basic obedience commands can be a surprisingly easy and fun task. Set aside a few minutes each day to work on training, and always finish up with a brief play session as an extra reward. In the beginning, five-minute training intervals are a practical goal. You may gradually increase this duration, but be careful not to exceed 15 minutes per training session. If you wish to spend more time on training, increase the frequency to two or three times a day instead of training for longer periods of time. By making training fun and keeping sessions brief, you ensure that your Papillon will approach training time with the exuberance that fosters success.

Another ideal way to maintain your dog's positive attitude toward training is by utilizing what he already knows. For example, if your Papillon has learned a special trick or a simple command, make a habit of bookending your training sessions with it. You can substitute new commands for this one as your dog's repertoire grows, but always remember to praise him for his compliance—even when the command is an old standard. This will help expand his confidence so that he can approach new training tasks with greater enthusiasm. One of the things dogs love most is pleasing their owners. Give your Papillon the tools to do this, and he will continue to put his whole heart into learning new tricks.

Making Sure Your Dog is All Ears

A command consisting of a single syllable is often easier for a dog to learn than a longer one. For this reason, limit the commands you use to two syllables at most. Words ending in hard consonants are usually the most effective. If you plan to show your dog or enter him in other competitive events, using traditional commands is best. If advanced training activities

Watch Those Hands!

Whenever you work on training your Papillon, be aware of what you do with your hands. Dogs pay attention not only to their owners' words, but also to their body language. For this reason, it is especially important that you use the same gestures whenever working on a specific command with your pet. If you raise your hand showing your dog your palm whenever you instruct him to stay, for example, you mustn't do this when you issue any other command. If you get your signals crossed, it could interfere with your dog's training success.

Learning basic obedience skills will make your dog better behaved and more confident.

aren't part of the picture, however, substitute your own words and phrases for the more conventional ones. One of my dogs, for instance, responds better to the word "wait" than the word "stay," perhaps because of the hard "t" sound at the end of the former command. Whatever words you choose, be consistent. Using two different commands for the same activity will only confuse your pet.

Also, avoid using your dog's name in conjunction with commands. If you say, "Max, sit!" your dog may respond, but will he associate his name with this activity? If so, this could confuse him when you later say, "Max, come!" Even more importantly, never use your dog's name along with the word "no" or as part of a reprimand, or he may form a negative connotation to hearing you say his name, even under more positive circumstances.

Sit

The *sit* command is the basis for many others, so it is a wonderful starting point for all future training. Even the youngest puppies are often capable of learning it.

Holding a treat, place your hand just above your dog's nose. As your dog moves his snout toward the treat, lift your hand

The sit *command is the basis for many others, so it is a wonderful starting point for all future training.*

slightly up and over his head and say the word "sit." This will naturally encourage your dog to shift his weight onto his haunches, moving himself into the sitting position. Once your dog sits, open your hand and offer the treat.

You should practice the *sit* command in a variety of places, so that your dog is accustomed to sitting whenever and wherever you say the word. Be sure to spend at least some time working near the main entrance of your home because this will make it easier to get your dog to comply even with the excitement and distraction of a visitor's arrival.

Down

The *down* command follows the *sit* command. It can be especially useful for helping your dog stay out of trouble, particularly when a person or another dog is approaching.

With your Papillon in the sitting position, hold a treat in front of him and then slowly lower your hand in front of his paws as you say the word "down." When he lowers his body to get the treat, offer both the treat and verbal praise. Once your dog is easily moving into the down position as a response to your moving hand, start issuing the command just before you show him the treat. Gradually begin limiting how far you lower or extend your hand. This will help wean your dog from depending on the visual cue.

Stay

Successfully learning the *stay* command can actually save your dog's life. For example, using this command whenever your doorbell rings will prevent your dog from running out the open door. *Stay* can also be helpful when you are entertaining a visitor who is uncomfortable around dogs.

Once your dog can reliably sit when told, you can begin working on the *stay* command. Expect puppies to remain still for only a second or two at first, although this duration will increase over time.

After instructing your pup to sit, raise your hand in a stop-sign gesture while saying the word "stay." Take a step back, and then return to your dog, providing a treat and praise. Make sure your dog does not stand or move as you present the treat because this will reward the wrong behavior.

When your dog is able to stay for a few seconds, begin gradually increasing both the number of steps you take away from your dog and the amount of time before offering the reward. Your ultimate goal is for your dog to remain sitting and still for about a minute or two with you at least 10 feet (3 m) away.

Come

The best way to start teaching your puppy the *come* command is by praising him whenever he does it naturally. If you spot your dog in the act of coming your way, say the word "come" in an upbeat tone, followed by excessive praise. It is paramount that you never scold your dog after commanding him to come to you, no matter what he might have done. By following this very important rule, you ensure that he will always come to you when called, even when he may be in the midst of a scary situation.

When you are ready to begin working on this command more directly, make sure your dog is on a leash or that you have another individual available to gently lead your dog to you when necessary. Retractable leashes work extremely well for this purpose. Whether you prefer using a leash or a training partner, you simply must have a way of getting your dog to follow the command if he doesn't promptly do so on his own.

The Command – Compliance Ratio

When issuing a command to your Papillon, say the word or phrase once—twice at the most. If your dog does not comply, gently enforce the command. If you constantly repeat yourself without expecting your dog's cooperation, he may assume that he doesn't have to obey your order. He could also begin associating the command you are using with whatever action he is performing instead of complying. To avoid these things from happening, never issue a command you cannot enforce, and keep the command-compliance ratio as evenly balanced as possible.

The drop-it and leave-it commands can protect your dog from many dangers, such as eating something harmful.

Heel

You can begin working on the *heel* command as soon as your Papillon puppy masters the *sit* command. Begin by walking your dog on your left side with the leash in your right hand and a treat in your left. When you stop, say the word "sit." When he complies, reward him and say the word "heel." Then begin walking again, stopping periodically to practice this two-part exercise. Your ultimate goal is for your dog to comfortably walk alongside you, stopping whenever you do.

If your dog pulls while walking on his lead, the worst thing you can do is to pull him back toward you in response. All this will accomplish is teaching your Papillon that he can play tug-of-war with his leash. Instead, if your dog begins pulling, stop walking immediately and practice heeling. Instruct your dog to sit, reward his compliance, and say the word "heel." Begin walking again, but be sure to stop each time your dog pulls to discourage the behavior.

Drop It/Leave It

The *drop-it* and *leave-it* commands can protect your Papillon from any number of dangers, including choking and being poisoned. Drop it can also be helpful when playing fetch.

Using a favorite toy, encourage your dog to play with the item for a few minutes before you say "drop it." As you issue the command, gently remove the toy from his mouth. Praise him immediately for complying, and return the item to him so you can repeat this exercise. At first, your dog may not be happy about relinquishing the item. With a little time and a lot of praise, though, he will comply without any physical prompting.

Although similar to the *drop-it* command, the *leave-it* command works a little differently because you do not want your dog to touch the item in question in the first place. The best way to teach this command is also by giving your dog a favorite toy and encouraging him to play with it. After a minute or so, toss another favorite item in his general direction. If, as you hope, his attention is captured by this toy, immediately say "leave it" and use the leash to keep him from touching it. Again, eventually you won't need to physically prevent him from touching the second item, but for now you merely want to interrupt his natural tendency to investigate the tossed toy. Once your dog shows success with this, begin practicing the command when he is off leash.

CLICKER TRAINING

A great way to reinforce the commands you teach your Papillon is to utilize a clicker. This small plastic item can be found at virtually any pet supply store for a very nominal cost. Clickers are in fact so economical that you may want to pick up several so that you always have one handy wherever you go with your pet. Many come attached to coiled bracelets to make using them even easier.

As its name implies, a clicker is a device that makes a clicking sound when a trainer presses it. It must be clicked at just the right moment, however, to reinforce the proper behavior. For example, if you are teaching your Papillon the *down* command, you must press the clicker as soon as you have said the word "down" and your dog has complied, and immediately offer him a treat. If you press it and reward your dog while he is still standing or sitting, the wrong command will be reinforced. Likewise, you mustn't wait until your Papillon rises from the down position, or he will associate the wrong action with the command instead.

Adjusting Your Training Approach to Suit Your Dog

Training is definitely not a *one-size-fits-all* activity. The more you work with your dog, the more you will see how his individual personality (as well as your own) affects your success. Before a particular training technique works for your dog, you may need to tweak it a bit. One of my own dogs seemed to have a hard time learning the *stay* command until my husband began telling her to *wait* instead. In Molly's case, we think the hard consonant at the end of the latter word resonates with her better than the softer sound of *stay*.

You might not even know at first what it is about a particular method that is wrong for your pet. Listen to your instincts at these times, as in so many other areas of pet ownership. By paying attention first and foremost to our dogs' reactions, we learn what does and doesn't work for them. In many ways, they teach us how to train them.

Although this all may sound rather complicated, a little practice usually does the trick. Think of using a clicker as somewhat like learning to drive an automobile; once you become familiar with all the steps, it becomes much easier to execute them correctly—and without having to consciously do them in the right order, etc. One way to help ensure your own success is by starting with a task your Papillon already knows, such as sitting. This will help keep his behavior more predictable as you become more familiar with this training method.

Operant Conditioning

First used in the 1940s, clicker training is considered by many dog owners to be a more relaxed and fun approach than traditional command-based training. It is based on a proven scientific method of learning called "operant conditioning." By marking a desired behavior the instant it occurs with a sound and then a treat, the trainer reinforces the behavior instantaneously. As with other styles of positive training, punishment for failure is never used with clicker training.

Initially, your dog may be distracted by the sound of the click, thus interrupting the desired behavior. If this happens, remember the importance of timing with the clicker. This is much more important than the timing of the treat.

One of the biggest advantages to clicker training is that it helps you catch your dog doing the things you want repeated.

The theory is that, in time, your dog will begin showing you the desired behaviors on his own, expecting the click. At this time, you should begin offering a cue for your Papillon to connect with the behavior. When your dog responds to the cue, you can offer the click followed by a reward, but only if the behavior happens during or after the cue. So, even though this regimen doesn't focus on commands, you will still be able to train your dog to respond to your instructions.

Another important rule of clicker training is only clicking once (pushing in, then releasing) for every time your dog demonstrates a particular behavior. It is fine to click for a behavior that is only a step toward the final goal, though. This is actually the best way to move your dog closer to your objectives. Eventually, as each behavior is mastered, you will discontinue using the clicker for that task, and begin using it for a new one.

Clicker training is not rocket science, but it is a science—so an instructor can be extremely helpful in showing you the best ways to use this effective technique. Although it may seem counterproductive for a large group of people to gather and make clicking noises all at once, a dog's hearing is so much

Once the root causes of a problem behavior are identified, it can usually be controlled. For example, leash pulling is the result of insufficient training.

better than our own that he is surprisingly capable of discerning his owner's click from any other. Classes are offered in many areas for this kind of dog training.

PROBLEM BEHAVIORS

As a breed, the Papillon is not prone to any problem behaviors in particular, but any dog may develop mischievous habits if undesirable actions are not corrected as soon as they appear. No matter how severe the situation, however, ignoring the problem behavior is never the answer. Nearly every dog is capable of change if his owner approaches remedial training with love and consistency.

Although you might contemplate punishing your pet for bad behavior, it is best to avoid this route. Instead, focus on rewarding him for acting properly. Also, consider how much time you spend with your pet. Just like children, dogs will often seek negative attention if they feel this is their only option. You may find that adding just one more walk or play session to your Papillon's day makes a huge difference. In nearly all cases, it is best to ignore the problem behavior when it does occur and teach an appropriate behavior later on, since any reaction whatsoever to bad behavior will be taken as encouragement.

The first step in dealing with any problem behavior is ruling out a physical cause. Is your Papillon peeing on your carpet because your hectic schedule has pushed housetraining to the bottom of your priority list, or is he experiencing the urgency that goes along with a bladder infection? Is your dog acting aggressively because he is trying to assume the alpha role in the family, or is he in some kind of pain? Your vet can help you answer these questions and also assist you in finding solutions, whether the cause is a physical or behavioral problem.

Aggression

Canine aggression must never be tolerated. Although many factors can contribute to a dog's tendency to bite, there are no acceptable excuses. If there is only one situation for which obedience training is necessary, this is it. From their very first human experiences, puppies should never be allowed to bite— not even playfully. This includes nibbling on hands and fingers. Teaching your dog that you are his leader is the most important step in correcting aggressive behavior. If your Papillon is biting, it may also be wise to consider details such as where your dog sleeps, when he is fed (this should always be after the people in the household eat), and what games you play with him—and how these things may be affecting your dog's perception of his place in the family.

To help prevent problems with aggression, always handle your dog gently. Your Papillon's mother may have carried him by the scruff of his neck as a puppy, but an adult dog can be injured if an owner picks him up in this way. Also, avoid playing games that pit your dog against you, such as tug of war, and never allow aggressive behaviors to be part of play. Growling, for example, may seem harmless, but it lays the foundation for your dog to bare his teeth in a more threatening way at other times. Aggression is a problem that can rapidly intensify. Consistent training is the best proactive step you can take to help your Papillon understand his place in the household.

If your Papillon has already assumed the alpha role in your household and uses aggressive behavior toward family members as a means of retaining this position, this is a true emergency. Consult your veterinarian, a canine obedience instructor or dog trainer, or an animal behaviorist immediately for advice on how to solve this very serious problem. The fact that your Papillon

Social Butterflies

Socializing your Papillon puppy is one of the most important aspects to training your new pet. Few things will affect his future experiences as much as exposing him to both people and fellow animals as early and as often as possible. Dogs who are constantly kept separate from others do not learn how to act properly around them. When faced with new visitors to their homes or unfamiliar animals at the park, these dogs may become frightened or aggressive. Fortunately, socialization is also one of the easiest things you can do for your Papillon. Simply bring him with you wherever you go whenever possible. Always bring along tasty treats for others to offer him, and he will instantly begin to equate people with rewards.

Of course, you must be respectful of those who do not wish to socialize with your Papillon. This means asking before you allow him to approach either a friend or a stranger. Also, for the sake of your dog's safety, always make sure that another animal is friendly before permitting interaction between the two. Just one oversight can leave both physical and emotional scars on your beloved pet.

Providing your dog with outlets for his energy may help prevent him from behaving inappropriately.

weighs only slightly more than a bag of sugar does not mean he is incapable of hurting someone, and you could be faced with a lawsuit, or worse, the unimaginable possibility of being legally forced to euthanize your dog.

Perhaps your Papillon shows no aggression toward you, but he bares his teeth whenever a stranger approaches him or members of his family. This was a problem I faced with my dog Jonathan. He was as amiable as could be with those he knew, but if Johnny was in the car with me, I had to lower my car window by just inches so I could pass the money through to the gas station attendant whenever I filled my fuel tank.

If your Papillon acts similarly protective over you, the best thing you can do is put him down on all fours and start obedience training him at once. Involving friends and family members in your pet's training may also be advantageous because this will help teach your dog that he must respect all people, not just you. Always carry treats and encourage new people to offer them to him regularly, since socialization will also be helpful. Most importantly, never assume that your Papillon's mildly aggressive behavior cannot escalate to a dangerous level just because he is small—it most certainly can if you don't take steps to keep this from happening.

Digging

If you think only large dogs dig, you may be surprised one day to find a tiny pile of dirt in your backyard after your Papillon is left there unattended for too long. Yes, even diminutive dogs dig. Because this is not only common but also normal, one of the best ways you can respond to digging behavior is to set aside a special area specifically for the activity. Your dog is small, so this solution may be much easier for you to manage than it would be if you owned a Saint Bernard or a Labrador Retriever.

Whenever your dog starts digging in an unacceptable area, such as near your flowers or vegetable garden, redirect him to his own space. Praise him for his compliance, but continue to keep an eye on him. Giving your dog some turf of his own is just one step in keeping digging a positive release instead of a problem behavior. You must also be sure the designated area is safe for your pet. Digging should never be allowed near fences or other areas where escape could result.

Excessive Barking

Whether the offender is a 150-pound (68-kg) Newfoundland or a 10-pound (5-kg) Papillon, excessive barking is one of the most nerve-wracking habits any dog can develop. Even if the sound of your dog's barking is music to your ears, it will almost certainly annoy other household members or neighbors. To avoid complaints from those individuals or visits from the police, you must put a stop to excessive barking.

If your dog is left alone regularly for long periods, he may bark or howl as a means of passing the time, or he might bark in response to noises he hears from outdoors. It may be wise to change his environment while you are away. Correcting this problem could be as simple as making small changes, such as leaving the radio or television on or making sure your dog has plenty of entertaining toys. If the situation does not improve, enrolling your dog in day care may be the answer.

If your Papillon barks excessively mainly when in your presence, effectively teaching him the *enough* command can solve

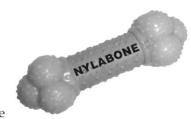

No Yelling!

Never yell at your dog when he barks. In addition to scaring him, all you will do by raising your voice is confuse him. To dogs, yelling sounds like barking. If you yell, your dog will think you are joining him in this vocal activity instead of understanding that you want him to stop.

If your dog barks when no one is at home with him, the problem probably stems from loneliness. In the wild, dogs vocalize as a way of bringing the pack together. Domestic dogs also use this technique to reach out to their human family members. One way to keep your dog from feeling lonesome is by taking him with you when you go to places where dogs are welcome. Of course, there will be times when your dog cannot accompany you, but being able to go along as often as possible can ease your dog's feelings of loneliness when he must remain at home.

To make the time your dog spends home alone more enjoyable, invest in some fun toys and yummy treats that he only gets when you are out. These can serve as practical distractions and can also help him form a more positive emotional response to being home without company. Some owners find that leaving a radio or television playing helps to ease boredom, another common factor for dogs who bark excessively when left by themselves.

NYLABONE

the problem. Begin by either waiting for your dog to bark or by making a noise to elicit the behavior. With an edible reward in hand, allow him to make noise for a moment or two, waiting for a break in the sound. As soon as your dog stops barking, say the word "enough" as you offer him the treat. As long as he does not return to making noise, praise him. Many owners find that using a clicker also helps with this task immensely.

Most owners don't mind when their dogs bark to alert them to strange noises or approaching visitors. In fact, many owners see this forewarning as part of a dog's responsibility as a pet. Although few people seeking a watchdog gravitate toward toy breeds, tiny dogs can be better than closed-circuit cameras in this way. If you don't want to lose this quality in your Papillon, you must not punish him for barking, but rather reward him for complying when you ask him to stop. Think of the *enough* command as a way of telling your dog, "Okay, I see what you are showing me. Now you can be quiet."

Inappropriate Chewing

Like barking, chewing is a natural canine behavior. When chewing becomes a problem, the solution is finding acceptable items for this healthy activity, not trying to stop it altogether. Puppies in particular need to chew as a means of dealing with the pain of teething. But even adult dogs should be provided with plenty of chew toys in a variety of textures and shapes, such as the ones made by Nylabone. In addition to affording your pet with a fun pastime, chew toys can save your delicate possessions from the wrath of your puppy's razor-sharp teeth. If you don't confront this issue when your dog is young, both his chewing and your frustration over it will likely increase.

Whenever you catch your dog with an inappropriate item in his mouth, take it away gently and replace it immediately with one of his toys. If he readily accepts this new item, lavish him with praise. You might even reward him with a fun play session to reinforce his positive association to this plaything. If he does not seem interested in the toy you offer, continue offering different objects until you discover one that does grab him.

Whatever you do, never offer your dog one of your own belongings as a toy. Whether you no longer have a need for a particular item or your dog has already ruined it, relinquishing it to him will only blur the lines between appropriate and inappropriate choices. The difference between your brand-new shoes and a pair scuffed to oblivion may be clear to you, but the leather will undoubtedly taste the same to your canine companion.

You can further help your Papillon by pet-proofing your home. Keep as many tempting items out of his reach as possible, a relatively easy task considering your dog's size. If your dog has set his sights (and his incisors) on your furniture or another item too large to be raised off the floor, consider treating the item with a bitter-tasting spray or a little lemon juice mixed with water to discourage chewing. Another great tool for preventing inappropriate chewing is your dog's crate. Use it whenever you cannot watch your pet properly.

Jumping Up

If you allow your Papillon to jump up on you or others in your home, this behavior can quickly turn into a habit. Although your toy dog probably won't hurt anyone by doing this, it may nonetheless be bothersome to your guests, especially those who are fearful of dogs. Because your dog is so lightweight, you may be tempted to interrupt his jumping by picking him up in your arms. Unfortunately, all this teaches him is that jumping up is a fast track to getting attention.

If your dog jumps out of excitement when greeting people, you can actually use his enthusiasm to your advantage in correcting the behavior. Simply invite one of his favorite guests over to practice the arrival scenario. Beginning with this person on your doorstep, instruct your Papillon to sit before you open the door. If he moves onto his feet while greeting your guest, this is fine, but if he jumps up at all, make sure your friend discontinues any attention she is giving your pet as you again command him to sit. A great way for your guest to interrupt the jumping up pattern is to move out of the way as soon as your dog's paws leave the floor. If your dog becomes extremely excited, you may find the *down* command helps squelch his urge to jump up from sitting. Ask your guest to join you in praising your Papillon for complying with your commands. This will show your dog that proper behavior—not jumping—is what leads to the attention he wants.

Marking Behavior/House Soiling

If your Papillon begins regressing in his housetraining, the problem could be house soiling. Sometimes called marking behavior, this habit of urinating for the sake of identifying territory with scent can be discouraged in a few ways. First, have your dog spayed or neutered. Although this may not solve the problem entirely, it will reduce your Papillon's urge to mark territory significantly. Remember, the cost of spaying and neutering is less than having your carpets cleaned just once. Second, thoroughly clean the areas your dog has marked. Third, begin the housetraining process again. Finally, if the problem persists, consider taking your dog for obedience training. This can help him accept his appropriate position in the household and discourage him from focusing on marking his turf.

Ruling Out Physical Causes

Occasionally, a previously well-trained dog may begin relieving himself in inappropriate places due to health reasons. If your dog suddenly begins having accidents, the first thing you should do is contact your veterinarian. Incontinence is a symptom of many health problems, including kidney problems and diabetes. Your vet will need to rule these conditions out before suggesting a plan of action to remedy the housetraining setback.

Housetraining Regression

Occasionally, a dog who has previously mastered the housetraining process begins having accidents again for no apparent reason. If this happens to your Papillon, make an appointment with your dog's veterinarian to rule out a medical cause, such as a kidney problem or diabetes, since incontinence can be a warning sign of either condition. It is crucial that you make sure the problem is not physical before you decide how to approach the issue behaviorally.

Occasionally, a previously housetrained dog may begin relieving himself in inappropriate places due to health reasons.

Dogs are extremely sensitive to dietary changes. Any sudden changes can cause digestive upset. This can result in diarrhea or, occasionally, temporary loss of bowel control. If your Papillon has eaten something that didn't agree with him, he may not be able to make it to the appropriate elimination area in time. Do not scold him for this. Remedial training also shouldn't be necessary following an isolated incident. If the problem is ongoing, however, have your dog checked by his vet.

Discovering blood in your dog's stool can be frightening, but chances are very good that the problem isn't as bad as you fear. Although in humans this is often a sign of serious illness, bloody stool is surprisingly more common in dogs. It does, however, signal a problem, so a veterinary exam should be scheduled. Your vet can determine if your dog is suffering from a parasite, an infection, or perhaps a more serious condition such as colitis. Often, bleeding is a result of a swallowed foreign object that has scraped the inside of your dog's large intestine.

Whether your dog is trained to defecate indoors or outdoors, regularly check his stool during the cleanup process. This can alert you to a health problem as early as possible. Contact your vet if your dog has passed bloody stools, dark, tarry-looking stools, or stools containing visible worms or other parasites. You will likely be asked to bring a stool sample, which you can carry to the office in a zip-style plastic bag.

Blood in urine is also a cause for concern and warrants a trip to the veterinarian. Although pink or red-tinged urine is usually a sign of a bladder infection, it can also be a symptom of a more serious problem, such as bladder cancer. This is a case in which having an accident indoors can be a blessing, since owners who walk their dogs may never have noticed the blood otherwise. If possible, bring a urine sample with you to the vet. This should be a free-catch sample, which means it has been collected in a small container (a clean baby food jar, for instance) directly as the Papillon urinates. Although this may sound difficult, another symptom of a bladder infection is frequent urination often accompanied by great urgency, so multiple opportunities to collect samples should present themselves.

Submissive Urination

Be careful you don't confuse submissive wetting or excitable wetting with intentional urination because these are not housetraining issues. Some dogs tend to leak urine at certain times, such as when their owners arrive home. Often they will lie down exposing their bellies in the process. This is done to show the owner that the dog knows his place in the pack and that he sees his owner as the superior dog.

You can minimize these kinds of accidents by ignoring your Papillon whenever you enter your home. Although it may seem harsh, avoiding an immediate greeting will help your dog retain control of his bladder. When you do greet your dog, avoid high-pitched tones because they can also elicit overexcitement. Avoid being too boisterous with both your voice and your movements, since either can draw out submissive behaviors.

Adding Another Dog

Because most Papillons are very social, adding a second dog to your family can be a great way to help ease any separation anxiety issues your pet may have. Nothing occupies a Papillon's time better than a friend just like him. Another Papillon is an ideal playmate for this breed, but your list of choices doesn't end there. Papillons also get along well with many other toy breeds. Do be careful, though, if you decide to add a bigger dog to the family. A Golden Retriever or even a Cocker Spaniel could inadvertently hurt your Papillon just by trying to play with him.

You also must have the time and financial resources to care for an additional pet. You won't notice a large increase in your weekly dog food bill, but veterinary costs for two dogs can be expensive. Most importantly, be certain that adding a second dog is right for you. Every dog you own should be equally wanted and cherished as a part of the family.

Some problem behaviors, such as separation anxiety, are caused by loneliness, fear, or stress.

Never scold a dog for these kinds of accidents. In the case of submissive wetting, it can actually make the problem worse.

Separation Anxiety

Howling or extended barking when your dog is left at home alone can be a tricky problem scenario. Most domestic dogs often howl only when prompted by a specific sound, such as a siren, but in the wild dogs howl as a means of bringing the pack together. If excessive barking or howling only occurs when your dog is left alone, this may signal a deeper problem of separation anxiety. If ignored, separation anxiety can further present in the form of chewing, housetraining regression, and sometimes even self-mutilation. One indication that you are dealing with an issue of separation anxiety is finding that treats you offer your dog before leaving home frequently remain uneaten.

Common Underlying Causes

The most common underlying causes of canine separation anxiety are confusion, fear, and stress. A variety of issues could be at the root of the problem. Perhaps your dog was taken from

his mother too early, a common occurrence at puppy mills. Maybe your dog's previous owner abandoned him at a shelter, leaving him especially fearful of your leaving him now. Maybe you have returned to work full time after taking a few weeks off to spend with your new puppy. This is another situation in which teaching basic obedience skills can help your dog become a more confident, less anxious being—the key to helping this condition.

Spend quality time with your Papillon regularly. Take him for walks often; regular exercise can significantly reduce his stress. Provide your dog with a crate for security, and follow the protocol of slowly introducing it while you are at home. If you cannot seem to correct the problem, consider enrolling your Papillon in day care or having someone else take care of him when you cannot be there. Even having a dog walker stop by midday may offer just enough of a break from the solitude to help your dog cope with being alone while you are away from home.

Trash Picking

If your Papillon has a penchant for trash picking, the solution is as simple as taking out the garbage. Avoid putting tempting items in trash containers within your home. Always use the garbage disposal for discarded food, and keep your wastebasket lids closed at all times. If your dog is particularly persistent in his dumpster diving, keep trash containers in closets or cupboards to limit his access.

Scavenging is a natural canine behavior, but some of the items your pet seeks out may surprise you. My own dog Damon has never once gotten into my kitchen trash can, but he will inevitably tear a tissue to shreds if he sees even a corner of it protruding from the bathroom wastebasket. For this reason, I have to be especially diligent about emptying my own trash containers—and I never put anything in them that could hurt my pets. Disposable razors, for instance, might not be what Damon is looking for, but he could be seriously injured if he ever encountered one while tearing up those tissues.

Compound Problems

Sometimes a dog displays two or more problem behaviors simultaneously. For instance, your Papillon may be barking excessively, chewing inappropriate items, and getting into your trash. If this scenario sounds familiar, ask yourself when these misbehaviors are occurring. If your dog acts out most often when you are not home, he may be trying to tell you that he is bored or lonely. Although the problems may seem numerous, a common solution may be the answer—such as keeping a wide variety of toys on hand or adding another Papillon to your home. Sometimes multiple problems require individual solutions; in these cases, the advice of a professional may be necessary.

How to Find a Behaviorist

The work of an animal behaviorist involves observing, interpreting, and modifying animal behavior so that she can help clients solve their pets' most serious behavior problems. The biggest difference between behaviorists and other animal trainers or instructors is the severity of the problems they address. Dog trainers and obedience instructors help owners prevent negative behaviors before they become serious issues. They may also work with owners to correct mild problem behaviors. Behaviorists, on the other hand, deal with more substantial matters. For example, the advice of a behaviorist may be necessary if your dog suffers from acute anxiety or phobias, aggression, or other behavioral disorders. In most situations, conventional trainers are not qualified to deal with these issues.

Like dog trainers and obedience instructors, behaviorists do not need any form of licensing to do their work, so careful selection is a must. Although a certification process does exist, there are currently only a limited number of certified behaviorists. You can find a directory of these individuals at www.animalbehavior.org. Although what is most important is that you are comfortable with the individual you choose, you should also seek a person with a certain level of education and experience dealing with animals, particularly small dogs. Having a degree in animal psychology or zoology is a definite advantage. The person also should possess dog training knowledge and experience. References from former clients are good, but recommendations from veterinarians and humane societies are even better. If you cannot find a certified behaviorist in your area on your own, these are the best resources that may lead to finding a reliable one.

ADVANCED TRAINING
and ACTIVITIES
With Your Papillon

O ne of the greatest things about dogs is how they bring people together. Have you ever noticed how you can strike up a conversation with a complete stranger in the middle of a pet supply store just by asking about her pet? I can't tell you how many times a quick stop for dog food has turned into a lively 20- or 30-minute discussion with another dog lover about our favorite topic: our animal companions.

Organized activities are an excellent means of meeting fellow Papillon enthusiasts. In addition to being fun for you, these pastimes are also great ways for your Papillon to socialize with other dogs and people as he gets to show off all that he has learned in a particular form of training. As an added benefit, many advanced activities provide pets with wonderful opportunities for exercise.

The very first Papillons I ever came face to face with were part of an outdoor conformation event held one summer in Cumberland, Maine. At the time, my son was only four years old and very eager to visit with these striking little dogs as soon as we saw them. I immediately told him that he had to ask before he patted the ones who were playing together in an x-pen during some down time, but before I could even get the words out, their owner was telling me, "He can pat them! Go ahead. It's good for them." Of course, she stayed with us the entire time and told us all sorts of interesting facts about her favorite breed, but this experience was just as beneficial for my son as it was for the dogs. He was able to practice all the skills his father and I were instilling in him relating to the proper way to treat animals. Now, several years later, he still remembers this woman's willingness to include him in this fun afternoon, which was part of his lifelong exposure to dogs.

CANINE GOOD CITIZEN® TEST

One of the best platforms for any advanced training activity, and truly an accomplishment within itself, is the completion of the American Kennel Club (AKC)

Canine Good Citizen (CGC) program. A certification series begun in 1989, the CGC program stresses responsible pet ownership by rewarding dogs who display good manners, both at home and in the community. Those interested may attend the CGC training program, an optional class offered to owners and their dogs, before taking a detailed 10-step test. Upon completion, certificates are awarded.

The CGC program focuses primarily on a dog's obedience skills and temperament, but it also stresses the importance of serious owner commitment. All owners are required to sign a Responsible Dog Owners Pledge before taking the test. This unique document states that the owner agrees to effectively care for her dog for the rest of the animal's life. It also encompasses such important areas as health and safety, exercise and training, and basic quality of life. It even addresses such community-based issues as agreeing to clean up after your dog in public and never allowing your dog to infringe on the rights of others.

A dog who passes this valuable examination is awarded an AKC certificate complete with CGC logo embossed in gold. CGC certification can also be useful to your dog in many other areas of advanced training. A dog worthy of the revered title of Canine Good

AKC Canine Good Citizen® Test

Dogs must pass all of the following tests to receive the Canine Good Citizen (CGC) certificate:

Test 1: Accepting a friendly stranger

Test 2: Sitting politely for petting

Test 3: Appearance and grooming

Test 4: Out for a walk

Test 5: Walking through a crowd

Test 6: *Sit* and *down* on command; staying in place

Test 7: Coming when called

Test 8: Reaction to another dog

Test 9: Reaction to distractions

Test 10: Supervised separation

Source: The AKC Canine Good Citizen® Test evaluation criteria.

Citizen is considered a responsible member of his community, a community that includes both people and dogs he already knows and all of those he will encounter in the future.

Although dogs of any age may participate in the CGC program, puppies must be at least old enough to have had all necessary immunizations. To ensure that your dog's certification is reliable, it is strongly recommended that younger dogs who pass the test get re-tested as adults, since temperaments and abilities can possibly change during this formative period. All breeds (as well as mixed breeds) are welcome in the program.

OBEDIENCE

One of the best ways to foster a strong relationship with your dog is to participate in an organized activity together, such as obedience training. The very basis of obedience training, after all, is developing good communication with your pet. The better your Papillon learns to respond to obedience commands, the greater the chances he will listen when it truly counts. In the ring, this may mean he earns a prestigious title, but in the real world the prize could be much more precious. Commands like *come* and *drop it* could likely save your dog from serious injury or even death.

One challenge you may face is finding the right-sized equipment for your Papillon. Collars and leashes should fit properly. Also, if using food rewards, remember that these must also be smaller than standard-sized training treats. A good trainer should be able to help point you toward all the appropriate accoutrement.

The Papillon ranks as the number one toy dog in obedience, making it clear that this little breed is capable of truly big things. A dog begins competing in obedience in the novice class. This beginner level focuses on the basic commands that every good canine companion should know: heeling both on and off leash at different speeds, coming when called, and staying for fixed periods of time. Upon compliance with the *stay* command, the dogs are simultaneously expected to remain still and quiet with a group of other dogs. Standing for examination by the judges is also a requirement.

After the novice class, the next phase is the open class. This second level of obedience competition is also called the

The foundation of obedience training is developing good communication with your dog.

Companion Dog Excellent (CDX) class. Many of the commands used in this sophomore stage of obedience are the same as in the novice class, but the dogs are expected to perform them off lead and for longer time periods. Jumping and retrieving tasks are also added to this phase.

Dogs nearing the top level of obedience strive for a Utility Dog (UD) title. This involves more difficult exercises prompted by hand signals and scent discrimination tasks. Once a Papillon has mastered this level of obedience, he may then move on to pursuing the highest obedience titles possible: Obedience Trial Champion (OTCH) and Utility Dog Excellent (UDX). These are both extremely venerated titles, and achieving them often takes both hard work and a considerable investment of time.

THERAPY WORK

Whenever I think of animal therapy work, I am instantly reminded of a visit my mother and I received from a therapy dog while my father was undergoing surgery a few years ago. Alone in my dad's hospital room, awaiting word from the doctor, we were nervously trying to pass the time with idle conversation when a beautiful German Shepherd appeared in the doorway. His owners, a retired couple, told us his name was Max and asked if we would enjoy spending some time with him. Although Max was already lifting our spirits, our immediate response was to tell the dog's owners that the patient had already been taken to surgery. Fortunately, neither the couple nor Max were deterred by our lack of understanding. As we soon learned, therapy dogs visit hospitals, nursing homes, and other facilities for both patients and families alike.

The amount of time Max spent with us on this day was short—just a matter of minutes, but the effects of his visit lasted well throughout the day. It enabled both my mother and me to relax for a bit and focus our attention on something positive instead of our worry. When my father finally moved from the recovery area back to his room with us, even he was able to benefit from the visit—just from our telling him about Max, whose official name was Olbs vom Huhnegrab.

German Shepherds have long been among the breeds used as working dogs, and therapy work has certainly been no exception to this, but more and more often smaller breeds like the Papillon are also being utilized for this important task. Because Paps are so tiny, they are sometimes less intimidating to people in the throes of a medical crisis. Like countless other small breeds, Papillons often make excellent therapy dogs.

If you think you and your Papillon would enjoy therapy work, your dog must become certified before you begin volunteering. Therapy Dogs International, Inc. (TDI), an organization founded in 1976, certifies, insures, and registers therapy dogs for this purpose. The first step in becoming certified by TDI is passing the Canine Good Citizen (CGC) test and getting the CGC certificate. This is not a guarantee that your dog will be accepted into a therapy program, but the social skills necessary for this achievement are an excellent indicator that your dog is a worthy candidate for the job. Some dogs fail the CGC test on their first attempt; if this happens to your dog, it doesn't necessarily mean the end of the road to therapy work. Dogs who are poorly suited for the pastime are typically identified rather quickly, but it usually takes more time to confirm that a particular dog is indeed right for the job.

Watch your Papillon when he is dealing with different people to judge which particular groups he appears to enjoy spending time with the most. Some dogs favor children, while others seem to delight in spending time with senior citizens. Some have a flair for communicating with the mentally ill. I strongly recommend scheduling your dog's volunteer time with the specific group of people to which he is most drawn. Not only will he be able to enjoy his work more this way, but he will also have the greatest effect on those he visits.

DOG SPORTS

Involving your Papillon in a sport can be a clever way to make playing with your pet take on a whole new meaning. Perhaps your dog is as quick as a bullet when he chases his ball and loves learning new things. If so, flyball may be just the thing for him. Do you find your Papillon jumping over obstacles in his path just for fun? Consider involving him in agility. Even playing some of these games in the privacy of your backyard can be exhilarating for your pet. You don't even have to enter him in formal competition if you don't want to—although it might be a whole lot of fun!

Agility

When compared with activities like obedience and conformation, agility is a relatively new canine pastime.

Developed in England during the 1970s, the sport wasn't recognized by the AKC in the United States until 1994. Resembling equestrian jumping competitions, it is

Choosing an Activity for Your Dog

How do you know which activity your Papillon would enjoy the most? Ask him! Of course, he won't be able to articulate his answer in words, but he will surely demonstrate a love, or distaste, for a particular activity once he is exposed to it a few times. You can get a feel for your dog's potential in obedience, for instance, by attending a basic class with him. Likewise, you may be able to assess his interest in agility by taking him to events where other dogs are competing.

Occasionally, a dog may excel at more than one organized activity but will usually gravitate toward a specific pastime. Limiting your pet's involvement in organized activities to just one or two types can also prevent him from becoming overscheduled. Not unlike a child, your dog should always approach his extracurricular activities with enthusiasm. Taking occasional time off from his sports activity schedule will help maintain his interest when it's time to head back into the ring.

Active, athletic, and highly trainable dogs, Papillons have shown exceptional abilities in dog sports such as agility.

conducted on courses built to a smaller scale but consisting of very similar pieces of equipment. Dogs must navigate jumps, vaulted walks, seesaws, Λ frames, and tunnels. They must be at least 12 months old to compete in agility, but this is one of the few limitations associated with the sport. Dogs of all breeds and breed combinations are eligible to participate. Owners are also given a bit more leeway here than in other types of competition; they are free to cheer their dogs on and run alongside them as they move through the different stations, offering verbal commands, hand signals, or a combination of these.

Like obedience, agility offers a beginner level, called the novice class. Succeeding at this level will earn your Papillon the title of Novice Agility Dog (NAD). Subsequent titles are then available in the following order: Open Agility Dog (OAD), Agility Dog Excellent (ADX), and Master Agility Excellent (MAX). The first three titles are achieved by earning qualifying scores in the respective class on three separate occasions and from two different judges. To earn the MAX title, however, a dog must earn ten qualifying scores in the Agility Dog Excellent class.

Weighty Issues

If your Papillon is carrying extra pounds, participating in an organized activity like agility or flyball can help lower his weight to a healthier number. Physical exercise is in fact just as important as lowering an overweight dog's calories when it comes to weight loss. You must make the transition from sedentary lapdog to star athlete gradually, though. Simple actions such as jumping can cause torn ligaments and other injuries in heavier pets. Before assembling those colorful tunnels and vaulted walks, discuss your new undertaking with your dog's vet. She can tell you how intensely and how often your dog should be exercising during the beginning phase of his new fitness plan.

Canine Freestyle

If you and your Papillon enjoy moving around to music, musical freestyle may be just the sport to provide both you and your pet with a fun opportunity for exercise and entertainment. Led by the World Canine Freestyle Organization (WCFO), this sport is relatively new, but it has been catching on all over the world for the last couple of decades. There are two basic varieties of freestyle—musical freestyle and heelwork-to-music. The former version consists of carefully choreographed musical programs in which both the owner and dog dance together. It involves precise teamwork, athleticism, and even costumes for both participants. The latter version incorporates traditional canine obedience skills into the routine. Both require an intense level of creativity and a willingness to let loose and have fun.

Although freestyle is very much a form of individual artistic expression, rules dictate what is and isn't allowed in competition. Likewise, a very specific point system is followed for judging. A 35-page list of these guidelines is available at the WCFO website at www.worldcaninefreestyle.org.

Freestyle is truly an event for the whole family. An owner may compete in canine freestyle with either one or two dogs. Two people may compete together with their canine duo in a pairs event, or participants may compete together in teams of three or more people and an equal number of dogs. A junior division also is available for kids under 18 years of age and dogs under 6 months, as well as a senior division for people 65 and older and dogs 9 years and up. There is even a division for mentally and/or physically handicapped dogs and their owners who may be similarly challenged.

The best way to learn about canine freestyle is by attending an event. Many offer instructional workshops for those interested in becoming involved in this fun new sport.

Like the recent inclusion of ice dancing in the winter Olympics, acceptance of canine freestyle as a bona fide sport among dog enthusiasts is still in its early stages. Many owners who prefer more traditional sports such as flyball or agility may scoff at dogs and owners jitter-bugging their way across the dance ring, but it's clearly those participants who are having the most fun. Watching a freestyle competition can also be great fun for onlookers. You will be truly amazed at what some of these

Playing It Cool

Always bring along fresh drinking water for your Papillon whenever you travel to an event. Because so many organized activities are held in the summertime, dehydration and heatstroke are always lurking dangers. It is vital that your dog stays hydrated, whether you are there to compete or just watch the event from the sidelines.

Additionally, no matter how much water you give your dog, you should never leave him alone in an automobile—not even for a short time. The interior of a vehicle with closed windows can reach upwards of 130°F (55°C) on a hot day. If you leave the windows open, you risk your pet's escape or theft. You could even face a fine for leaving your Papillon alone in your car. In Florida and California, for instance, there are laws against leaving a pet in a closed vehicle.

dogs and their owners can do. To learn more about freestyle, contact the WCFO at www.worldcaninefreestyle.org.

Flyball

Flyball is an exciting canine sport that requires both speed and dexterity. Upon hearing a signal, a dog is released onto the flyball course, which is a small and straight strip of land. His goal is to run over four hurdles to the end of the course, where a box with a trap and foot lever awaits him. The dog then jumps onto the foot lever, releasing a tennis ball into the air. After he leaps to catch this ball, he darts back to his owner with it. This is all timed down to the second. Typically, flyball is a team sport consisting of two to four relay teams of four dogs per team. Dogs may compete on either single-breed or multi-breed teams, and even mixed-breed dogs are eligible to participate.

Flyball is a particularly fun pastime for dogs ready to take regular ball playing to the next level. Although larger dogs tend to dominate in this sport, smaller breeds are welcomed onto multi-breed teams with great enthusiasm because the height of the hurdles is set according to the height of the smallest dog on the team. Little dogs also often clock impressive times, despite the fact that they need to use much more of their power to trigger the ball release.

Walking/Jogging

Although Papillons can be impressive athletes, it is

Sports and Safety

When it comes to sports, your dog's safety must always be your first priority. Because so many canine sporting events are held outdoors, always carry fresh drinking water for your Papillon, along with a container from which he can drink. Also, watch your pet for signs that he needs a break. During practice time, this means stopping whenever you notice your pet panting excessively or showing other signs that he is tired. For competition, this means allowing him adequate time to rest before taking his turn. Additionally, be sure to warm your dog up before he performs any intense physical activity. Just like people, our pets can overexert themselves when not properly conditioned for exercise.

usually better to stick with walking your dog instead of making him your jogging partner. Because this breed is prone to knee problems, the stress of running for long periods can be particularly problematic, especially in younger dogs. Just as you should limit your precious pet's caloric intake, you should also keep physical exercise at a reasonable amount and intensity level. In addition to injuries, overexertion can cause low blood sugar, seizures, or even a heart attack. If you are a runner, the best way to involve your Papillon in your hobby is to incorporate him into either your warm-up or cool-down period.

Never underestimate the benefit of a good walk. Regular walks can fulfill the majority of your dog's exercise needs. Of course, there is a difference between walking and strolling. When walking with your Papillon, start slow and gradually increase your speed until you are moving at a brisk pace. Watch your dog for signs that he needs to slow back down, and opt for multiple short trips rather than one long one each day.

If you walk your dog to provide him with an opportunity to relieve himself, try to head in a different direction for this task. Using a separate leash for the two activities can also help your dog differentiate walking for fun from walking to do his business. Papillons are amazingly intelligent animals. Tap into this potential to get the most out of your every trip outdoors.

COMPETING IN MULTIPLE EVENTS

Can your Papillon compete in more than one advanced activity? The short answer is yes. There are no rules stating that a show dog cannot compete in obedience, or that an obedience competitor cannot participate in agility. Many dogs participate in two or more advanced training activities without a problem. Some dogs, along with their owners, thrive on involvement in a variety of challenging activities.

Others insist that one activity frequently can interfere with or limit a dog's success in another. A dog who has gone through a painstaking process to achieve titles in obedience, for instance, may have a hard time adapting to the innate freedoms of agility. Another dog with a similar past could take to agility quite well, but regress in his mastery of obedience, while yet another may succeed in both activities equally well.

Regular walks can fulfill the majority of your dog's exercise needs.

You know your dog best. If you think you both might enjoy a new activity, try it. You are always free to take a break from one activity and then come back to it if a new one ends up not being the one for you and your Papillon. The most important thing is that both you and your dog are having fun. Do be careful, though, not to over-schedule either yourself or your dog. These activities, while serious in nature, are meant to be enjoyable. If they start feeling like obligations, or if your dog seems to be losing his fondness for them, it may be time to think about reducing the number of events you attend regularly.

GAMES

Papillons love playing, and given the chance most will spend countless hours doing just that. A very active breed for its size, the Papillon celebrates the beginning of play time by doing what many breeders call "zoomies"—a series of energetic laps around the yard. "It's rather comical to see," one such breeder confided to me.

Another favorite Papillon pastime is playing ball. Because the breed is so intelligent, an owner can create many variations to

Many dogs participate in more than one advanced activity without a problem.

this age-old game. Your Papillon's mouth is very small, however, so you must choose a ball of appropriate size. The best way to play ball with a Papillon is by bouncing the ball gently away from the dog and allowing him to run after it, or by rolling it slowly toward him.

Fetch

Fetch is a game that can be played with any toy your Papillon fancies. Keep in mind, however, that your dog might not be especially keen on giving up a particularly treasured item once he has taken possession of it. This can be part of the fun for your dog, but discontinue play if his possessiveness escalates to aggressive behavior.

Follow-the-Leader

Many Papillons are naturals at follow-the-leader. Using various kinds of impromptu obstacles, this game can easily be played in a backyard or inside the home using furniture, hallways, and other items within your home as props. Placing a reward such as a favorite toy or other treat at the end of the course can be a fun addition.

Hide-and-Seek

Playing hide-and-seek is a great way to practice the *sit*, *stay*, and *come* commands with your Papillon. After giving the first two commands, find a place to hide and then call your dog. Remember to reward him for finding you. You can also hide a treat for your dog to find. As your Papillon becomes more adept at locating the treat, try hiding additional treats. This lays the groundwork for a treasure hunt.

Tricks

Teaching your Papillon tricks can be a fun way to incorporate training into play time. A Pap can easily be taught the "give me five" gesture (hitting the person's hand with his paw), to turn in a circle, or to jump up in the air. Maybe you prefer tried and true favorites, such as shaking hands or speaking (barking on command), or perhaps you want to make up your own tricks as you go along. When it comes to tricks, the possibilities are only as endless as your imagination.

Playing With Toys

Finally, don't forget toys! Toys can be a great motivator to get your dog moving. Saving one or two special items for more active play times helps ensure that your dog will be willing to participate in a good old-fashioned game of fetch when the time comes. Toys are also great nonedible rewards to use at the end of an informal training session. Chews and interactive toys, such as the ones made by Nylabone, offer a great way to enhance overall physical and mental fitness.

Believe it or not, some dogs can be taught to pick up and put away their own toys. A variation of playing fetch, this game of sorts can be a fun and useful way to cap off each play session. Like many other games, it can also be a great foundation for further training activities.

Nylabone

Seize the opportunity for play whenever your schedule allows. You don't need big chunks of time. Your Papillon will actually get more out of several shorter periods of play throughout the day than he will from one longer, exhausting session.

As with more organized activities, it is best to end games on a positive note. If you quit playing while your Papillon is still having fun, he will be more interested in joining in the fun the next time. This will help maintain your dog's attention if you do wish to incorporate training into future play times.

SHOWING YOUR DOG

The Westminster Kennel Club Dog Show is a big event in our home. Each year, my husband, our son, and I watch the televised coverage, celebrating each dog's win and making our own guesses for the top dog in each group beforehand. We marvel at all the breathtaking dogs, listen attentively for information about the more exotic breeds, and cheer on our favorite competitors. Inevitably, one of us announces how our own dogs are much cuter than the Best in Show winner at the end. Both our dogs were the pups of champions, after all. They could have been show dogs, too, right?

Although the excitement of conformation is certainly appealing, the truth is that showing is not for all dogs. Only dogs who most closely match their breed standard stand a chance in formal competition. What I am about to disclose is difficult for me, but I do so in hopes that I might encourage others to take this very important step. Even my own beautiful dogs are not perfect. This doesn't bother me, but hearing it from someone else would. This is why I have never considered showing them.

I picked out my dog Molly the day she was born. Unfortunately, I had to wait a while before I knew for certain I could indeed have her. At the time, my breeder wasn't planning to keep any of the puppies, but she had agreed to give the sire's owner pick of the litter. Some breeders will wait weeks or even months before deciding which, if any, puppies they wish to keep from their litters. It can take this long to tell if a particular dog has the characteristics that will bring him success in the ring.

Making Fun of Competition

The trick to making any advanced training activity a success is keeping the experience fun for both you and your dog. If either of you feels stressed or pressured, it can limit your enjoyment—and even hinder your dog's accomplishments. Keep this in mind when transitioning from your backyard to formal competitions. Although the rules may be a bit different in the new setting, your overall approach shouldn't change when you and your Papillon make this move. Remain positive, and you will always have something to celebrate on the way home.

You can learn about conformation by attending dog shows.

My breeder, who has since become a good friend, has told me on many occasions that Molly has numerous show qualities, but she also confided to me before I brought Molly home that her bite was a bit off. "You could still show her if you really wanted to," she conceded. "It's not a disqualification, but most people wouldn't show a dog with a bad bite." Secretly, I was relieved by Molly's misaligned teeth, since in the end they may have been part of the reason I was able to have her. She may not be perfect, but she is perfect for me. The term that breeders use for dogs like her is "pet quality," although I prefer to think of Molly as a "quality pet."

Is Showing for You?

Although many breeders prefer to keep their show-quality dogs, a fair number of breeders enjoy selling some of their near-perfect pooches to other Papillon enthusiasts who plan to show them. Be sure to tell your breeder that you are looking for a future show dog, and expect to pay a higher price for the puppy you ultimately choose. Although a breeder can point you toward a puppy with excellent show potential, however, know that there are no guarantees. You should be leery of anyone who makes promises for success in the ring. There is no such thing as a truly perfect dog of any breed. Even champions are dogs who most closely match their breed standard, a bar that is intentionally set extremely high.

Showing also requires a great deal of work and commitment on behalf of the owner. If you show your dog yourself, you must set aside a considerable amount of time for training, grooming, and attending events. Many events will require travel, especially if your dog excels in competition. You may utilize a professional handler, of course, but this can be expensive, and you must find someone whom you trust with your precious Papillon. Above all else, the dog you choose should be a treasured pet, no matter how many titles he earns in conformation or other organized activities.

What Happens at a Dog Show

If you have never attended a dog show, you have been missing out on one of the most enjoyable ways to learn about dogs. At these lively events, you will find knowledgeable breeders and handlers, other dog enthusiasts, and of course lots and lots of dogs. Specialty shows are conformation events in which all the entrants are dogs of the same breed. You can find these by checking with the nearest breed club. Multi-breed shows consist of various purebred dogs. Mixed breeds are not eligible for competition in either type of show. Also, because dog shows began as a means of evaluating breeding stock, only

Dress for Success

When showing your dog, dress neatly in comfortable attire. While you certainly want to look your best, you do not want to steal attention away from your dog—or worse, clash with his features. Opt for stretchy fabrics that will move with you as you escort your dog around the show ring. Remember, you may need to bend and kneel occasionally, so dresses and skirts are impractical. Pantsuits and split skirts are ideal for female handlers, while men may find that trousers paired with a tasteful blazer provide both comfort and versatility. Colors that contrast with your dog's coat often work best. If you spend most of your training time in jeans and t-shirts, take some time to select a dressier outfit for showing that you indeed feel comfortable wearing, and make sure it fits properly. Remember, you will have your picture taken if your dog wins!

At a show, dogs are judged against the standard for the breed.

animals who have not yet been spayed or neutered are allowed to enter AKC conformation events.

At a multi-breed show, dogs are divided into seven groups—the sporting, hound, working, terrier, toy, nonsporting, and herding group. Each dog is then placed in one of five classes: puppy, novice, bred by exhibitor, American-bred, and open. Males are always judged first. A member of the toy group, the Papillon is often a charming competitor both for his own group title and for Best in Show, an honor bestowed upon one of the group winners at the end of the event. Shows vary in size and variety from small, local events to national all-breed shows with more than 3,000 entrants.

How a Dog Becomes a Champion

Dogs accumulate between one and five points with each win. The number of points awarded depends on the number of dogs

AKC Ribbons

An AKC award-winning dog receives a ribbon from the judge that indicates what type of conformation award he has won:

Blue—first place in any regular class

Red—second place in each class

Yellow—third place in each class

White—fourth place in each class

Purple—Winner's Dog and Winner's Bitch classes

Purple and White—Runners-up in Winner's Dog and Winner's Bitch classes

Blue and White—Best of Winner's (chosen between Winner's Dog and Winner's Bitch)

Purple and Gold—Best in Breed in each competition

Red and White—Best of Opposite Sex (to Best in Breed Winner)

Red, White, and Blue—Best in Show

in competition, the location of the event, and several other factors. Shows awarding three or more points are considered majors. A total of 15 points is necessary for championship status. When a dog reaches this level, he has earned the title of Champion (abbreviated as Ch.) to be used before his name thereafter.

Although the Papillons competing in a particular show may appear to be extremely similar in appearance, there are always important differences between them. What might seem insignificant to spectators can appear glaringly obvious to judges, who look at every nuance of an individual dog to compare him with the breed standard. Dogs with faults are usually quickly eliminated, but better specimens rise to the top of the competition, making championship status a highly coveted distinction.

Characteristics of a Show Dog

In addition to being attractive, show dogs must possess very stable temperaments. A perfectly correct Papillon will not be tolerated in the ring if he acts aggressively toward the other dogs or people there. A show dog must also stand for a fair amount of probing when being examined by a judge. This can range from simple coat inspection to having his bite checked. Just a quick growl could cost him a win.

You may find that your dog simply does not have what it takes to compete in conformation. Show dogs must endure frequent travel, strangers (both human and canine), meticulous grooming, and the noise of crowds—and meet the aesthetic standards for competition. In most cases, unless you purchased a dog already designated as potential show material, the chances of your Papillon excelling in the ring are relatively slim.

If your dog is a poor fit for conformation, consider one of the other advanced training activities that may be a better fit for the two of you. The perfect show dog may be out there waiting for someone to buy him, but this Papillon is here now and needs your time and attention—and he just may be destined for greatness in another type of event.

HEALTH

of Your Papillon

At one time, providing canine health care simply meant bringing your dog to see a veterinarian once a year, typically whichever one was closest to your home. The better veterinary hospitals would mail you a reminder postcard a few weeks before your dog was due for this annual visit and inform you of any accompanying shots he required. There was never a question as to whether or not you would have your pet vaccinated, and holistic care was virtually unheard of. Certainly, the choices once made for a dog's diet, exercise schedule, and grooming routine impacted his health just as much as they do today, but topics such as food preservatives, dental hygiene, and specialized care were subjects never spoken about with vets.

Fortunately, contemporary veterinary medicine has evolved into a much more comprehensive form of pet care. It now consists of routine veterinary examinations, complemented by an ongoing dialogue you maintain with the qualified health care professionals you choose for your Papillon.

FINDING A VET

Once you decide to welcome a Papillon into your home, one of your first priorities is to find the best possible veterinarian for your new pet. The specific requirements that top your list may differ somewhat from those of someone who owns a larger dog—or even from those of a fellow Papillon owner. But what matters most is that you are comfortable with the person you choose to provide this care. If you don't trust your dog's veterinarian, it can make working together for your pet's health a difficult endeavor. Conversely, when you find one with whom both you and your dog mesh, it can make

Annual veterinary checkups are essential if you want your dog to stay healthy.

even a stressful health crisis an easily managed situation for all involved.

Getting Referrals

Although you can certainly find an abundance of names that include a D.V.M. suffix listed in the phone book or online, I recommend turning to more personal sources as a starting point for your search. Ask for recommendations from friends or neighbors who have pets. Your Papillon's breeder or a local humane society are also wonderful resources for this kind of information. You can further supplement your research on the Internet, but investigate further by calling to verify information, ask questions specific to your concerns, and request references.

What to Look for in a Quality Practice

Selecting a veterinarian is often a matter of individual preference, but there are a few universal considerations that all owners should take into account before scheduling an initial exam. First, does the vet have experience with toy breeds? Small dogs face different health problems than larger ones. Although canine veterinarians are trained to treat dogs of all breeds and sizes, having firsthand knowledge of Papillon health is a definite plus. I also like to ask what kind of pets a vet has at home. Although a cat lover can make a fine canine veterinarian (and vice versa), I feel more confident knowing that my vet has personal experience as a dog owner.

Additionally, request a tour of the facilities that includes a chance to meet with the vet and the rest of the staff. The veterinarian may be the one who signs the rabies certificates, but both you and your dog will also be dealing with office workers and technicians when visiting the hospital. Support staff members play important roles in your dog's care, often making the difference between a low-stress visit and a nerve-racking experience for your pet. These gatekeepers will also be your most important contacts in the event of an emergency. Observe the staff as they interact with other clients, and make note of any areas that may be a concern, such as poor attitudes or understaffing.

The facilities should be clean and comfortable, but they need not be elaborately decorated or filled with expensive furniture. Neither of these aesthetic luxuries have anything to do with superior care. Separate waiting rooms for those seeking routine care and those with sick pets are often a plus, though. Some hospitals even offer separate entrances for cats and dogs. There are occasions when little things such as these can make all the difference. My own vet now offers an entrance for clients arriving for their appointments and a separate exit for those whose exams are finished. If you could only see the signature on my cancelled checks from the days I had to simultaneously pay my bill and hold my dog's leash while trying to keep her away from the other dogs in the waiting room, you would instantly know how much more convenient this new one-way orientation is for me—and for the poor souls at the bank who once had to decipher my erratic scrawls!

If a particular hospital refuses to give you a tour, consider this a red flag. You should be able to schedule a tour at virtually any facility, although you may have to wait longer for a more convenient time. A great way to see if your planned visit matches up to a typical day at the hospital is to stop by in person to make your initial appointment. Bring along a list of questions, and be sure to listen to the answers carefully. Important issues include whether your Papillon will see the same vet for each and every visit, if the vet handles emergencies, and whether a staff member is available on-site after hours to monitor patients recovering from surgeries, especially when postoperative bleeding may be a concern. Responses should always be given in a straightforward manner. Keep in mind that no one—not even a veterinarian—should be expected to know the answer to every question you may ask, but she should always be willing to find the answer for you.

Emergency Care

Even if the veterinarian you choose handles emergencies, it is also wise to select an emergency veterinary clinic in your area. In the event that a problem arises when your vet's office is closed, you must know how to get to such a facility as quickly  as possible. For this reason, it is wise to not only jot down the address and phone number, but to also follow up by actually going to the clinic before an emergency

How Can I Be a Good Veterinary Client?

Learn what is normal for your pet so that you recognize the first signs of illness, and see your vet regularly for preventive visits, not only when your pet becomes ill. If a pet is not well, don't wait until he is really sick before calling your vet. It is frustrating for a vet, and heartbreaking to owners, to see an animal die of an illness that could have been treated successfully if professional care had begun sooner.

Schedule appointments, be on time, and—for your pet's safety as well as that of other clients and pets—bring your pet to the veterinary office on a leash or in a carrier. Even if you have an emergency, call ahead to ensure that the veterinarian is available. An emergency may occur when your vet is not available, so ask for a referral to an emergency veterinary facility.

Before it becomes necessary, take a practice drive to the veterinary office, since trying to find it when you really need it can cost precious minutes. Post the office's number near your telephone for quick access. Do not disturb your veterinarian during nonworking hours for matters that can wait, and do not expect your veterinarian to diagnose a pet's problem over the telephone.

(Courtesy of the Humane Society of the United States)

strikes so you won't waste time getting lost or finding out that the clinic has moved or isn't open at a particular time. Some emergency clinics are open 24 hours a day, while others operate only when traditional veterinary hospitals are closed.

If the emergency clinic isn't busy, go inside and request information. Many clinics offer pamphlets about their specific protocols and prices. Due to the nature of emergency care, a clinic of this kind often charges more than a veterinary practice offering general care. It may even require prepayment for a basic emergency examination. By knowing what to expect, you ensure that your Papillon will receive the medical attention he needs in a situation during which mere minutes can make all the difference.

PHYSICAL EXAMINATIONS

One of the first things that you should do after bringing your puppy home is take him to the veterinarian for a thorough checkup. If anything is wrong, you want to know about it as soon as possible. Should a serious problem be discovered, you will have to decide whether you will be able to face the associated care issues and medical costs of keeping him.

The initial checkup is just the beginning of the routine health care you will need to provide for your Papillon, however. Just because a dog is healthy doesn't mean that he won't benefit from regular well-dog veterinary visits. Prevention is always the best medicine, and it is usually at annual exams that a vet detects early signs of potentially serious health issues that can affect your dog throughout the various stages of his life.

The First Checkup

Your puppy's first checkup is an exciting event. It will likely be his first opportunity to meet the veterinary staff and to form early impressions of visiting this unknown place. Be sure to bring some treats with you for your Papillon. Although most hospitals keep goodies on hand, your puppy may be more likely to accept a treat from a stranger if it smells familiar. This small step can help him feel less nervous, and it can provide a huge leap toward socializing him.

At the beginning of your appointment, a veterinary technician will take you to an exam room and weigh your

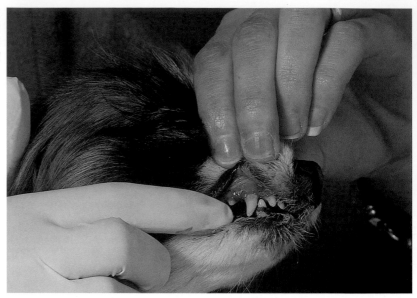

During your Papillon's first checkup, the vet will give him a thorough physical examination from head to tail.

puppy. You will be asked some general questions about his history and overall health. His temperature will be taken and recorded in a chart, along with any questions or concerns you may want to discuss with the vet. These may pertain to health, behavior, or even grooming. Your veterinarian is one of the best resources for information about virtually all areas of pet care. If she cannot answer a particular question, she should be able to refer you to someone who can.

A great way to make sure you don't forget any questions you wish to ask is to make a list before your appointment. Bring this with you, along with a pen so you can jot down any detailed answers, such as how much to feed your new puppy or the names and numbers of the best dog trainers in your area—after all, this information won't do your Papillon any good if you can't remember it.

After addressing your concerns and speaking with you about basic care, the vet will give your puppy a thorough physical examination from head to tail, which includes examining his eyes, ears, teeth, heart, lungs, and joints. Depending on your puppy's age, he may also be due for certain vaccinations. This initial appointment is also an excellent time to schedule spaying or neutering, unless you plan to show your Papillon in conformation.

Spaying and Neutering

Sometimes referred to as "fixing," sterilization is one of the most valuable decisions a dog owner can make. With this single choice, you are increasing your Papillon's potential life span, as well as helping to control the ever-growing unwanted pet population. With the number of animals entering shelters in the United States each year totaling upwards of six to eight million, this is a problem that demands every pet owner's attention.

Spaying, the proper term for sterilizing a female dog, involves removing the ovaries and uterus so she cannot become pregnant. Sterilization also eliminates the risk of ovarian and uterine cancers and uterine infections, and it significantly reduces the risk of breast cancer later in a dog's life. A spayed female will not go into heat, the state that immediately precedes ovulation in dogs. A female in heat will attract the attention of any male dogs nearby, and she will also bleed during this time.

Neutering, the equivalent procedure for males, consists of removing the testicles, and therefore the dog's ability to impregnate a female. This eliminates the risk of testicular cancer, and it is also significantly reduces the risk of prostate cancer. Neutered males also tend to exhibit fewer annoying behaviors, such as marking territory, excessive barking and howling, and aggression.

Both male and female dogs should be sterilized by the time they are six months old unless they will be shown or bred. Statistically, pets who are sterilized by this age live longer than intact dogs. Show dogs or dogs used for breeding should be sterilized after they no longer participate in these activities. Under normal circumstances, neither operation carries significant risk to the dog.

However, because of a Papillon's extremely small size, risks are associated with giving birth. Papillons are among those dog breeds that most often require emergency C-sections. Unless you have experience breeding Papillons, and your dog exhibits all the desirable qualities of the breed that should be passed on, it is best to leave breeding to professionals.

Annual Checkups

Your Papillon should see his veterinarian once a year for a wellness exam. This routine appointment will typically take

Bring a Sample

Take a fresh stool sample with you to your puppy's veterinary appointment. They'll need to check your puppy's feces for parasites. If you don't bring a sample then, they'll need to insert an instrument into his rectum to get one. That could be unpleasant and frightening for your puppy. Make it easier on everyone and bring a sample for testing.

A routine wellness exam typically takes about a half hour.

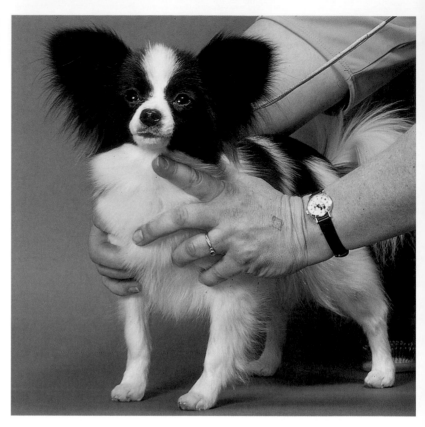

about 30 minutes. Even if your dog appears completely healthy, it is vital that he receives this routine checkup to make sure that everything is indeed as it seems. Dogs are amazingly resilient creatures. They often don't exhibit any symptoms until an illness has already progressed into a more serious situation. Many dangerous health problems can be identified and corrected during a regular vet visit, but you must provide your veterinarian with the opportunity to do so.

Increasing the frequency of your dog's routine exams to twice each year once he reaches the age of nine or ten is a smart precaution. Conditions that once may have presented only a minor obstacle to your pet's good health will now progress more rapidly. Early diagnosis is your best tool in winning the fight against virtually any affliction. Also, during these important visits, talk to your vet about adjustments in nutrition, exercise, and daily care that may help keep your senior Papillon feeling his best.

Vaccinations

Vaccinations have become a subject of increasing debate in recent years. Similar to concerned parents who elect to place their children on delayed vaccination schedules to minimize harmful side effects, pet owners too are weighing the risks associated with immunizations. If their dogs do not fall into a high-risk category for a particular disease, an increasing number of people are opting not to vaccinate for that illness. Vets and owners alike are also erring on the side of caution when it comes to the frequency of vaccinating and the number of shots a dog receives in a single vet visit. Over-vaccinating has been linked to thyroid disease, liver and kidney disease, and even cancer.

Whenever a vaccination is administered, it alters the immune system. Vaccinating a dog with an autoimmune disease can be particularly dangerous for this reason. If your dog has been diagnosed with an autoimmune disease, talk to your vet about getting a waiver for the vaccines that are required by law in your state. If your Papillon has received vaccinations in the past, your vet may even be able to use a titer (a blood test for antibodies) to show that your pet has already been sufficiently vaccinated for that particular illness.

Necessary Vaccines

All this being said, unless your dog suffers from an autoimmune disease, being cautious does not mean abstaining from vaccinating altogether. Vaccination can prevent many life-threatening diseases from striking your pet. Rabies, for example, is almost always fatal; the vaccination for this virus is required by law throughout the United States. Because studies have shown that the rabies vaccination remains effective much longer than previously thought, however, more and more states are lengthening the time between necessary booster shots. What was once an annual vaccine is now required only every three years. This same schedule is now typical for vaccinating against distemper and parvovirus, as well.

Optional Vaccines

So, which additional vaccines may be necessary for your Papillon? The answers depend on several factors, including his age and overall health, the climate in which he lives, and

Vaccinations help to protect your dog against many life-threatening diseases.

the areas to which he is taken on a regular basis. If you board your dog or take him to day care, for instance, the bordetella (kennel cough) vaccine may be a prerequisite to entrance. If, however, your Papillon rarely visits public places frequented by other dogs, you may feel comfortable skipping this shot because kennel cough is highly curable. Be sure to wait at least two weeks between vaccinations.

Getting Your Dog Vaccinated

If you find that making several different hospital appointments for vaccinations is too expensive, consider utilizing low-cost vaccination clinics. Many pet supply stores and animal organizations regularly hold these popular events. Just be sure to provide your veterinarian with copies of the paperwork you receive so that your dog's records remain current. You may also opt to administer some of your Papillon's vaccines yourself. By law, the rabies vaccine must be given by a licensed veterinarian, but other vaccines can be purchased from vet supply companies and administered at home. A third option is simply to ask your veterinarian if she would consider waiving the additional office visit fees after your dog's initial exam. Many vets are more than willing to work with their clients, especially when it benefits the animals.

Your Papillon's Vaccination Protocol

Sometimes making the decision whether to vaccinate for a specific illness is a tough one. Lyme disease, for example, is a serious affliction that can ultimately leave a dog unable to walk if left untreated. This might lead an owner to believe that vaccinating is the best choice. When Lyme disease is caught early, however, permanent damage can be avoided through simple treatment with an antibiotic. If you live in Maine as I do, vaccinating may still be the smarter option because 85 percent of Lyme disease cases are in the northeast and in Wisconsin. If you live in California, on the other hand, you may be more moved by the fact that none of the 27 veterinary colleges in the United States recommend vaccinating for Lyme disease.

Discuss vaccinations with your vet at your Papillon puppy's first appointment, even if your dog isn't due for any shots. The best way to make a decision about these or any other health issues concerning your pet is by arming yourself with as much reliable information as possible and giving yourself the time to choose the best course of action for you and your pet. What you decide this year may be entirely different from choices you make down the road as even more is learned about the vaccinating process. And remember to always observe your Papillon carefully in the hours and days following the inoculations he does receive. Any dog can experience an allergic reaction to an immunization.

COMMON HEALTH ISSUES IN PAPILLONS

There isn't a single dog breed that is not prone to at least a few specific diseases or genetic abnormalities. Although some breeds are certainly susceptible to more problems than others, no breed is entirely free of these kinds of issues. Fortunately, most Papillon-specific conditions are manageable, but good breeders take reasonable steps to help lower the risk of many of these afflictions in their litters. They not only have an obligation to remove afflicted dogs from their breeding programs, but they also have a responsibility to predict conditions that may likely beset certain dogs in the future and refrain from breeding those animals, as well. Genetic testing and certified evaluations are valuable resources in the breeding process for this reason.

Knowing how to recognize potential health problems and how to handle them is important to your dog's overall well-being.

Even the healthiest parents, though, can produce a puppy who will go on to experience one or more health problems as an adult. Your dog may never be confronted with any of the following conditions, but arming yourself with information about them will enable you to help him through whatever lies ahead.

Epilepsy

My Cocker Spaniel, Molly, began suffering from epilepsy when she was just two years old. Like Cockers, Papillons are also prone to this erratic illness, which oddly can be harder on the dogs' owners than on the animals themselves. Caused by a malfunction in the dog's brain, epilepsy is characterized by shaking, drooling, and loss of motor control. A seizing dog may also lose control of his bladder or bowels and appear completely unaware of his surroundings until after the incident has passed. Fortunately, most vets believe that this quasi-unconsciousness does indeed prevent the dog from experiencing the seizure as intensely as those who witness it.

If your dog ever seizes, the most important thing to remember is that staying calm will make this stressful event more manageable. Pay close attention to both the duration and frequency of each seizure. When episodes are minor and sporadic, treatment may not be necessary. If the seizures tend to last more than five minutes or happen as often as once a month, however, your veterinarian may suggest placing your Papillon on an anticonvulsant medication. As soon as each seizure ends, record as many details as you can remember and relay this information to your veterinarian so that together you can select the best treatment plan for your pet.

Idiopathic epilepsy is the diagnosis given when no particular cause of the seizures can be identified. This is most common in dogs under the age of five. Sometimes, however, epilepsy is secondary to another illness, such as liver disease, kidney disease, or cancer. For this reason, it is especially important that any dog who has suffered a seizure receive a thorough physical examination, complete with a blood profile. This could make all the difference in identifying the underlying problem and treating it before it is too late. Even when medication is necessary, epileptic dogs can still live surprisingly normal lives.

Hypoglycemia

Like other toy breeds, Papillons face an increased risk of hypoglycemia. The medical term for low blood sugar, hypoglycemia is essentially the opposite of diabetes. Most dogs outgrow the problem naturally before they are even old enough to leave their mothers, but in some cases the condition remains a continued threat to the dog's health. At times, it can even be brought on by stress.

Symptoms of hypoglycemia include poor coordination, weakness, and glassy eyes. If your dog exhibits these signs,

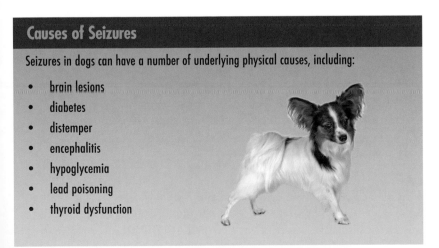

Causes of Seizures

Seizures in dogs can have a number of underlying physical causes, including:

- brain lesions
- diabetes
- distemper
- encephalitis
- hypoglycemia
- lead poisoning
- thyroid dysfunction

Like other toy breeds, Papillons face an increased risk of hypoglycemia. Symptoms include poor coordination, weakness, and glassy eyes.

the first thing you should do is feed him food with a high sugar content, such as corn syrup or honey. If the dog is especially weak, you may have to put a small amount on your finger and rub it on your dog's gums. Never try to force any food down your dog's throat because he could choke. If your Papillon readily accepts the treat and can sit on his own, offer him a small meal. The dog should also be kept warm. Next, contact your dog's veterinarian. Even if the episode passes easily with the help of a sugary treat, it is still vital that your vet knows about the incident. He will likely ask you to bring your Papillon in for an exam at this time.

Hypoglycemia is a very serious but manageable disease. If left untreated, however, a hypoglycemic dog can experience seizures, lose consciousness, or even die. Once the disease is diagnosed, you can control symptoms by feeding smaller, more frequent meals. It is especially important that a dog with this condition doesn't miss a meal, so make arrangements for someone else to feed your Papillon if you are ever unable to make it home in time. If you take your dog on regular walks, it may be a good idea to take along liquid glucose packets. These can be purchased at most pharmacies.

Your veterinarian can also help you select a food high in protein, fat, and complex carbohydrates to help your Papillon best utilize his nutrients. You will generally want to avoid feeding simple sugars, but you might need to adjust your dog's diet accordingly if his exercise level increases, because more frequent or intense physical activity may justify an increased sugar intake. Talk to your vet about the right plan for your dog.

Hypothyroidism

Middle-aged Papillons face an increased risk of an endocrine disorder called hypothyroidism. A dog's thyroid consists of two butterfly-shaped lobes located on the back of the neck. The hormone these lobes secrete is responsible for maintaining the body's metabolism (the rate at which the body processes its nutrients). In dogs with hypothyroidism, this gland is underactive, consequently decreasing your dog's metabolism and making it easier for him to gain weight. Most often a dog is predisposed to hypothyroidism. It is most common in larger breeds, but the Papillon and a few other toy breeds are also susceptible to the condition.

If your dog has put on some weight, don't immediately assume that the thyroid gland is the cause of the problem. If your Papillon's food intake has not increased along with his weight, however, you may want to look for other symptoms. Has your dog experienced any hair loss or dry skin? Does he always seem to be cold, seeking out warmer places to rest? Does he seem lethargic or depressed? Have ear infections been a problem? These are all signs that the weight gain may be related to a thyroid issue.

If you suspect that your dog is suffering from hypothyroidism, schedule an appointment with your veterinarian. Most dogs will show symptoms between the ages of four and ten. Your vet will use a series of tests to diagnose the condition. Once diagnosed, your Papillon will need to take a synthetic thyroid hormone to help adjust his metabolism. Periodic blood samples will then need to be drawn to assess the effectiveness of the treatment and to make any necessary adjustments.

Treatment is usually extremely successful. Most dogs treated for hypothyroidism return to their normal weight and activity levels quickly once treatment is begun. Although regular follow-up appointments will be necessary to monitor the hormone dosage, your dog should remain symptom-free for the rest of his life and will have the potential to live just as long as a Papillon without a thyroid problem.

Liver Shunt

Liver shunt is a serious condition that causes a dog's circulatory system to bypass the liver. Although not extremely

One Smart Cookie

If you have trouble getting your dog to swallow a pill, check your favorite pet supply store for special treats with hollow centers. This clever design enables you to hide your dog's pill inside, making medicating your Papillon as easy as feeding biscuits to a puppy!

common, this genetic disease appears to be on the rise in the Papillon breed. Intrahepatic shunts emerge on the inside of the liver, while extrahepatic shunts occur on the outside of the organ. In the latter condition, which is more common, surgical correction can be made to reroute the blood flow to the liver. Intrahepatic shunts, though, are considerably more difficult to reach and, therefore, to correct. When surgical intervention isn't possible (due to either limited availability or expense), the condition may be managed successfully with medication and diet.

Patellar Luxation

Like many small breeds, Papillons are susceptible to patellar luxation. This condition, aggravated by excess weight, involves the dislocation of a small, flat bone at the front of the dog's knee. This loose kneecap can slip out of place either occasionally or frequently, making it difficult for the dog to place any weight on the affected leg. If you see your dog hopping around on just

Bone and joint problems can be very debilitating, so care should be taken to prevent accidents and injuries.

three legs, a luxating patella (sometimes referred to as slipped stifles) might be the problem.

Once your veterinarian has confirmed this to be the problem, she may suggest the use of an anti-inflammatory drug. If the problem persists, however, surgery may be necessary. As with other skeletal problems, arthritis may also develop as a result of this condition.

Because patellar luxation is usually caused (and definitely intensified) by the impact from falls, it is particularly important that you not allow your Papillon to jump from high places. This includes tall furniture and stairs. Younger dogs, whose bodies are still growing, are especially susceptible to this kind of injury, so keep a close eye on puppies.

Periodontal Disease

Because anesthesia is best avoided whenever possible, proactive dental care is a must for this breed. With their tiny mouths and lips lying so close to their teeth, plaque and tartar accumulate extremely quickly without regular brushing. Tooth loss is very common in dogs as young as four years old when this simple step is neglected.

Periodontal disease begins with a condition called gingivitis. The most obvious sign of this is bad breath. At first, your dog may not feel any discomfort, but soon the redness and swelling that characterize the illness become apparent, making it difficult for him to chew bones and even eat the crunchy foods that help keep plaque and tartar from forming on his teeth.

Once periodontal disease sets in, options are limited. A professional cleaning can reverse the condition in the earliest stages when consistent dental hygiene is regularly performed at home, but extraction is usually necessary once a tooth has begun to decay. If you notice a small amount of plaque on your dog's teeth, you may find it helpful to purchase a tooth scaler. This inexpensive tool can help you avoid having to schedule a cleaning, but don't rely on it too heavily because scaling without polishing can leave scratches on the enamel surface. If you find yourself scraping your dog's teeth on a regular basis, this is a sign that you should be using his toothbrush more often.

NYLABONE

Progressive Retinal Atrophy (PRA)

Progressive retinal atrophy (PRA) is an inherited disorder that causes gradual but inevitable vision loss. This is caused by the deterioration of the retina. A dog with PRA will begin bumping into things only at night or in low-light situations, but will eventually show signs of increasing vision loss regardless of the time of day or light quality. Although PRA has additional symptoms (including dilated pupils and hyperreflectivity, or shininess, to the back of the eye), these signs are rarely noticeable until the disease has already reached an advanced stage.

If PRA has a positive side, it is the amount of time that an owner is given to help prepare for her dog's eventual sight loss. Although it is natural to feel overwhelmed at first by the prognosis of permanent blindness, it is important to realize that your Papillon will be impacted by this deficit far less than a human being in a similar situation. Blind dogs can live enormously satisfying lives. Although some additional training will be necessary, most sightless dogs acclimate to this change easily by simply doing what they have always done: rely on their other, more valued senses, particularly hearing and smell.

If your dog is faced with PRA, give yourself some time to accept this unexpected turn of events, but know that the ordeal won't be nearly as dreadful as you might fear. After an initial adjustment period, both you and your dog will be able to enjoy a surprisingly normal life together despite your pet's visual impairment.

Reverse Sneezing

When your Papillon becomes extremely excited, you may observe a strange phenomenon most commonly referred to as reverse sneezing. The technical term for this snorting-like sound is inspiratory paroxysmal respiration. Put this way, it sounds like a dangerous condition (and the noise itself can be a bit alarming for the uninitiated!), but fortunately this common occurrence caused by spasms in the trachea isn't harmful to your pet. You must be certain, however, that you rule out a more serious cause for the sound, such as choking. Because reverse sneezing can also occur when a dog with a dry throat swallows a treat, there may be a moment of panic for both owner and pet if these two events occur simultaneously.

Although there is no way to prevent reverse sneezing, remaining calm during an episode can help make it pass much more quickly. Massaging your Papillon's throat gently will encourage him to swallow and stay calm himself. If this doesn't work, cover your dog's nose briefly (no more than a few seconds) to prompt him to breathe through his mouth. Another technique heralded by breeders is placing a treat in your hand and allowing your dog to nibble at it slowly until the snorting has stopped.

As you spend more time with your new Papillon, you will become familiar with the sounds that are normal for him. If you are concerned that he is experiencing reverse sneezing too frequently, discuss the issue with your veterinarian. Although this is usually a harmless condition on its own, it can sometimes be a symptom of another problem, such as a soft palette or soft trachea.

Sensitivity to Anesthesia

There is always a certain amount of risk associated with anesthesia. For this reason, preventive health care is preferable to having your dog require procedures for which he must be anesthetized. In the past, toys breeds have faced particular dangers relating to anesthesia, but newer inhalant anesthetics (such as isoflurane) have lowered these risks considerably. Whenever possible, postpone elective procedures until your dog needs to be anesthetized for another more pressing reason.

Also, you can lower your dog's risks by having your veterinarian run blood tests before a surgery to identify any health problems that could be exacerbated by anesthesia. Another important factor to consider is your Papillon's weight because obese dogs face significantly higher risks of complications, such as cardiac arrest and poor circulation of oxygenated blood to the tissues when under anesthesia. Owners of overweight dogs often find themselves having to put off even medically necessary operations until their pet loses enough weight to make the use of anesthesia safe.

Obesity and Anesthesia: A Compound Problem

Toy breeds in general face increased risks from certain types of anesthesia, but for overweight Papillons, even the surgery itself can be dangerous. Layers of superfluous fat on such a small dog can make it more difficult for the veterinarian to see what she is doing during a surgical procedure. Additionally, an obese dog's liver can take much longer to break down the anesthetic. This means it may take the dog longer to regain consciousness. Because the liver must break down the anesthetic and any other necessary drugs, recovery also can be delayed as a result.

Hip dysplasia, an inherited defect, can occur in small breeds like the Papillon. Severe cases can make moving around difficult for your dog.

OTHER COMMON HEALTH PROBLEMS

A number of health problems are a concern for all dog owners due to their prevalence within the canine species.

Allergies

Just like humans, dogs suffer from allergies. Also similar to the problem in humans, identifying canine allergens can be rather time-consuming. Although allergy tests are available, often the most effective route is good old-fashioned trial and error.

Many pets suffer from food-related allergies. If your Papillon's tummy seems to be consistently upset by his food, begin removing as few ingredients at once as possible (ideally, just one at a time) and watch for any physical reactions. If no improvement is noticed after several days, return that item to your dog's diet and remove another until you can isolate the problem-causing agent. Common canine food allergens are corn and wheat, but because every dog is different, the problem could be almost anything. The best way to avoid this painstaking identification process is to introduce new foods to your dog slowly and one at a time.

Other common canine allergies involve skin reactions. If your Papillon experiences severe itching, redness, or a rash, schedule an appointment with your veterinarian to determine the cause. Make note of when the problem first appeared and any other symptoms your dog may also have because this information can help your vet diagnose the problem.

Hip Dysplasia

When many of us hear the term hip dysplasia, we immediately think of larger breeds such as Labrador Retrievers, but this problem can occur in smaller breeds as well. A malformation of the ball-and-socket in the hip joint, hip dysplasia is an inherited defect that usually isn't evident until a dog is between six and eight months old. Although the condition may be mild, moderate, or severe, the signs are usually the same, including lameness, stiffness, and limping. Symptoms may be intensified on cold, damp days. A dog suffering from hip dysplasia may also exhibit an understandable change in temperament.

With time, the pain and the problem may seem to dissipate, but more likely this is simply the result of scar tissue that forms from the stretching and tearing of the joint. Eventually, arthritis also sets in, and the painful symptoms return.

Diagnosis is made through veterinary examination and X-rays. A veterinarian may recommend surgery in extreme cases, but medical treatment is also possible. This may include enforced rest periods during times of acute discomfort, weight control, mild analgesics (pain killers), and anti-inflammatory drugs. Although surgical treatment may seem like a risky endeavor, many dogs return to a full activity level, even after having a full hip replacement.

Internal and External Parasites

Parasites live on or in the body of animals and obtain at least a portion of their sustenance from their hosts without providing any benefits in return. They can seriously compromise the health

Natural Flea Prevention

A number of natural alternatives are on the market for flea prevention and treatment, but they may likely fall short of completely solving the problem. Garlic and brewer's yeast, the two most common repellents of this kind, have not been proven to control fleas, but many owners who prefer a nonchemical approach insist that they do make a difference. Always consult your vet before giving your pet any flea treatment—even when the ingredients are considered natural. Remember, just because a substance is natural, it doesn't mean that it isn't harmful. Large doses of garlic, for instance, can be dangerous to dogs because garlic is a member of the onion family.

Always check your dog for fleas and ticks after he has spent time outdoors.

of dogs, especially in the case of puppies, who do not have the bodily reserves to counteract the detrimental effects of parasites.

Parasite control is not only necessary for the health of your dog, it is also important for you and your family because some parasites are easily transmitted to humans. Prevention and prompt treatment for infestations can keep your entire household healthy.

Fleas

Few things are as exasperating as fighting a flea infestation. Because these most common pests to dogs live and feed solely on the exterior of their hosts, fleas are considered ectoparasitic. The good news is this makes it possible for owners to detect their presence before they can cause an internal problem, such as anemia or tapeworms.

Dogs with fleas scratch excessively, particularly around their tails and thighs. Another sign of infestation is something called flea dirt (pepper-sized feces), which can be found in your dog's coat using a flea comb. How do you tell the difference between feces and true dirt? Clean the comb with a damp paper towel. If the debris turns red (from digested blood), your dog has fleas.

For insects that cannot fly, fleas can move impressive distances—as much as 150 times their body length in a single jump. Perhaps even more striking, though, is that a single adult female flea has the ability to lay 30 to 40 eggs per day. This makes it imperative that you treat not only your dog, but also his environment thoroughly. Eggs can continue to hatch throughout the winter season inside your home.

The best way to prevent fleas from taking up residence on your Papillon and inside your home is by giving him a monthly preventive. This medication is administered topically to the back of your dog's neck, after which it spreads progressively over the rest of the body's skin surface. Because the ingredients are not absorbed into the bloodstream, the medication is only toxic to fleas. Do wash your hands thoroughly after treating your dog, though, and avoid touching the application area until the solution has had a chance to spread thoroughly. This treatment rids your dog of any existing fleas within hours and also prevents future infestation. Flea preventives can be purchased at either a vet's office or various pet supply retailers.

You may also ask your veterinarian about which products to use to treat the inside of your home. Because you are dealing with highly toxic chemicals, read labels and follow directions carefully. Most important, remember to remove all people and pets from the home before treating it. Also, remove all kitchenware and utensils, including your dog's dishes, and store them behind closed doors. If your home is carpeted, make sure to vacuum repeatedly after a flea infestation and dispose of the bag immediately whether it is full or not.

Check with your vet before using any over-the-counter flea or tick product. Organophosphate insecticides (OPs) and carbamates are found in various products and should be avoided because they pose particular health threats to children and pets even when used correctly. A product contains an OP if the ingredient list contains chlorpyrifos, dichlorvos, phosmet, naled, tetrachlorvinphos, diazinon, or malathion. A product contains a carbamate if the ingredient list includes carbaryl or propoxur.

Puppies can be severely affected by internal parasites.

Ticks

Ticks can carry some of the most menacing diseases in existence today, including ehrlichiosis (a bacterial infection), encephalitis, Rocky Mountain spotted fever, tick paralysis, and perhaps the best known ailment of the bunch—Lyme disease. One of the best ways to tell a tick from less harmful insects is by counting its legs. Being an arachnid, a tick will have eight legs, while an insect will only have six. Unlike most insects, ticks attach themselves to their hosts with great force, often making removal difficult.

Many ticks are extremely small and can therefore be extremely difficult to see in their normal state. For example, an adult deer tick (which spreads Lyme disease) is about 2.5 mm—about the size of a sesame seed. Once a tick attaches itself to a chosen host, however, it begins engorging on the host's blood. An adult Rocky Mountain wood tick is typically between 2.1 and 6.1 mm in length, but can measure as much as 16.5 mm when engorged. The longer a tick is attached to your dog, the more engorged it will get, but you want to find and remove any tick that attacks your pet as soon as possible to avoid infection.

If you find a tick on your dog, grab a pair of fine-pointed tweezers, some isopropyl alcohol, and a pair of latex gloves. With the gloves on and using the tweezers, very slowly grasp the tick and pull it gently from your dog's skin. Be careful not to pinch your dog, but do get as close to the skin as possible. If you pull too quickly or use a twisting motion, you may separate the tick's body from its head, which can remain imbedded in your pet. Some sources suggest using a drop or two of isopropyl alcohol to get a tick to release its stubborn grip, but according to the American Lyme Disease Foundation, this method can backfire or even increase the chances of disease transmission. If you cannot get the tick to release, or if you remove only part of it, seek assistance from your veterinarian.

Once the tick is removed, drop it into some alcohol to kill it. Never use your bare hands because any infection could then pass to you. As soon as the tick has been disposed of, clean the bite wound with disinfectant and sterilize the tweezers with fresh alcohol.

The same monthly treatment you use to prevent fleas from accosting your Papillon should also prevent ticks from attaching themselves to your pet. Because owners can sometimes forget to administer this medication on time, however, it is still a wise idea to check your dog regularly, especially if you live in a high-risk area of the country, such as New England. If you take your dog for frequent walks in the woods, doing a tick check should become a standard part of your routine. It is important to note, however, that ticks are not restricted to the woods and high grass. They can also frequent suburban backyards or public parks.

Heartworm Disease

Heartworm is a devastating illness that can lead to heart failure, as well as liver and kidney damage. Treatment can be successful if the illness is diagnosed early, but prevention is highly preferable and also amazingly simple. At one time, heartworm, a parasite passed from host to host through the bites of mosquitoes, was believed only to affect dogs in southern climates. As temperatures have continued to rise in so many areas around the world, though, the number of heartworm cases in untreated animals has also risen. It now occurs throughout the entire United States.

A monthly preventive medication is all that's necessary to keep this horrible disease from striking your Papillon. Owners living in the northern United States may opt to treat their dogs only during the warmer months of the year. After all, you don't see too many mosquitoes in the middle of the winter, right? But you may be surprised to learn that mosquitoes can survive temperatures as low as 57°F (14°C). By continuing the monthly preventive throughout the winter season, you can virtually ensure that your pet won't contract the illness even if temperatures remain unseasonably warm. Year-round treatment will also help thwart intestinal parasites, which can infect people as well as pets.

All dogs should be tested for heartworm disease prior to beginning a preventive regimen. Your veterinarian can check your Papillon for it with a simple blood draw. In previous years, results typically took a few days, but contemporary versions yield answers in just a few minutes. This makes prevention even easier because owners must receive a negative result before beginning certain preventives.

Worms

Recently, a friend of mine experienced an incredibly scary incident involving her beloved dog, Baylie. For two full weeks, Baylie suffered from intense, bloody

Deworming Caution

Internal parasites that may infest your dog are commonly referred to as worms. Thirty-four percent of dogs in the United States are infected with some kind of gastrointestinal parasite. This is why many breeders and rescues have all their dogs dewormed whether they show signs of being infested or not. Because the problem can return, however, you must always be on the lookout and bring stool samples to your vet regularly. Although the presence of certain types (such as roundworms and tapeworms) can easily be seen in your dog's stool, diagnosing others (such as whipworms and hookworms) can be more difficult. Signs of worms include excessive licking of the anal region or dragging the rear end.

Never give your dog a dewormer (medication intended to rid a dog's body of worms) without the prior approval of and instructions from your vet. If your dog does become infested with worms, seek treatment at once (don't forget to bring that stool sample) and be sure to follow up by treating his environment to prevent further infestation.

diarrhea. The vet, after examining her and running tests, informed my friend of the various possibilities, cancer being one of them. This was especially frightening since Baylie had already battled this illness (successfully!) twice. In the end, the culprit turned out to be hookworms.

Hookworms are tiny parasites that attach themselves to the wall of a dog's small intestine, where they begin sucking his blood and laying eggs. Baylie likely came into contact with hookworms through infected soil while walking in the Maine woods, one of her favorite pastimes. If she had been a puppy at the time she was infested, the situation could have been deadly. Fortunately, even a chronic case of hookworms isn't usually fatal in adult dogs, but prompt diagnosis is imperative. This is done by examining feces for hookworm eggs under a microscope. Diarrhea is just one symptom, however. If your dog has been infested, he may also experience weight loss, anemia, and progressive weakness.

Other worms that may sicken your Papillon include roundworms, tapeworms, and whipworms. Because roundworms are capable of growing as long as several inches (several cms), they may be seen in vomit or stool without the aid of a microscope. Also due to their size, these worms can cause an intestinal blockage, a potentially fatal situation. Adult dogs can be infested with active roundworms, or they can harbor encysted worms that become active during pregnancy. Dams can pass them on to their unborn puppies, even if they have been dewormed themselves.

If you notice debris resembling grains of rice in your Papillon's stool when cleaning up after him, he may have tapeworms. These small, flat worms may also be found in the hair surrounding your dog's anus. Tapeworms usually strike dogs who have ingested fleas, another important reason for  flea prevention. Unlike other worms that commonly infest dogs, tapeworms cannot be killed by most over-the-counter dewormers, so again, you must seek veterinary care.

Of all these internal parasites, whipworms, which are not visible to the naked eye, can be extremely difficult to detect, sometimes requiring several checks before a definitive diagnosis can be made. They are long, thread-like parasites that are thicker at one end. They live in a dog's cecum, the pouch that forms

Types of Intestinal Worms

The following intestinal worms can cause major problems for dogs:

- heartworms
- hookworms
- roundworms
- tapeworms
- whipworms

Some of these worms are visible to the naked eye, while others can only be detected under microscopic examination—a good reason to have your veterinarian check for them at your dog's annual veterinary checkup.

the beginning of the large intestine. Symptoms include anemia, weight loss, flatulence, diarrhea with blood or mucus in the stool, and lack of energy.

Like other canine health problems, it is best to prevent a worm infestation, but giving deworming medication without knowing the worm status of a healthy dog is not a good idea. Always contact your veterinarian before giving your dog a vermicide. Mixing dewormers or administering them with other medications can be dangerous. The best way to prevent worm infestations is proper cleanup. This means removing feces from your yard (and all public places) as quickly as possible, ideally as soon as your dog eliminates.

I recommend bringing a stool sample with you each time your dog has a veterinary exam. Although some dogs drag their behinds on the ground or floor in response to itching caused by worms, the best way to confirm parasite infestation is to have your dog's stool examined by a vet. Quite often, worms or worm eggs are visible under the microscope when there are no obvious signs of infestation. Regular checks ensure that you uncover a problem before it becomes serious. If your dog is diagnosed with worms, you must treat both your pet and his environment. Many parasitic worms can infect people as well as pets, and the effects can be extreme.

Ruptured Cruciate Ligament

The anterior cruciate ligament (ACL) is a vulnerable part of a dog's body. Usually, the first indication of the problem is that a dog with a ruptured ACL will abstain from resting his weight on the injured leg. Another sign is that he will tend to extend a rear leg when he is in a sitting position. If the meniscus (cartilage disk in the knee joint) has been torn, a popping sound may be heard when the dog walks. There may also be pain and swelling at the joint. Although the lameness may subside after awhile, it is likely to return because movement causes further damage.

When my dog experienced this problem, acupuncture worked well as a therapy, but it isn't necessarily the best choice for all dogs. Selecting a treatment plan for any affliction is a decision you should make with your veterinarian based on the individual details of your Papillon's situation. Friends whose dogs also encountered this problem chose surgical correction instead. Their pets enjoyed the same level of success as my dog. It is important to note that if the affected knee is left untreated, the effects of arthritis will be greater once it sets in, and surgery may be less effective if performed at this point.

Massage: A Hands-On Approach to Wellness

Similar to human babies, dogs benefit from human handling, especially in the form of massage. In addition to making your Papillon feel good, giving him regular massages can increase his flexibility, reduce pain, and increase circulation. It can also have a calming effect on an anxious animal. The most important thing to remember, though, is that your dog must be receptive to the process. If he resists, stop at once. Massage should never be uncomfortable or stressful for your pet.

Massage your Papillon by gently stroking his body in a single direction in long fluid motions; this approach, which warms the body tissue, is known as effleurage. Your dog may likely respond by leaning into your hand or even lying down; these are both signs that your dog is enjoying himself. Continue stroking your pet for as long as he appears receptive. A smart approach to use on a dog new to massage is something called passive touch. This nearly weightless technique involves applying no pressure whatsoever, just the lightest possible caresses. Once your dog acclimates, you can then move on to other methods, including drumming, kneading, rolling, and stretching.

Ask your veterinarian which of these is best for your dog. She may also suggest an instructional book or video about canine massage to you. In addition to strengthening your dog's body, you may also deepen your relationship with him by utilizing this timeless therapeutic technique.

COMPLEMENTARY MEDICINE

At one time, veterinary care consisted of merely showing up for an annual checkup, during which the vet asked a few quick questions and gave your dog "his shots." With the possible exception of rabies, many owners didn't even know which diseases these inoculations prevented. If a more serious problem arose, medication would be prescribed, or surgery would be scheduled. Veterinary diagnoses were much like early computer programs: if a dog was itching, then flea powder was recommended. A plus B predictably equaled a go-to statement that led to C.

As people have become more receptive to nonconventional approaches to their own medical care, however, we have likewise turned to alternative treatments for our pets' health. Discussions with our veterinarians now include a range of topics relating to general pet care, lifestyle, and our dogs' emotional well-being, as well as their physical health. We look at the whole picture, the very basis for holistic medicine. (The word holistic in fact means whole.)

While some owners might think of complementary modalities (sometimes called alternative medicine) as trendy or desperate, these methods actually date back thousands of years, with impressive success rates. Chinese acupuncture, for example, is an ancient form of healing involving the precise placement of hair-thin needles into various parts of the body to stimulate healing and overall good health. It has been shown to help with such ailments as arthritis, epilepsy, and even cancer. It can also relieve pain and strengthen the immune system.

Homeopathy, another ancient holistic medicine, is the very root of modern-day vaccinations. The premise of this technique is that by introducing an infinitesimal dose of a particular disease-causing agent into the body, we can stimulate a natural immunologic response, effectively arming the body for future exposure to the agent. One must be extremely careful when using this treatment method because the tenet of this modality is that the smaller the dose, the more powerful the effect. Only trained professionals should be allowed to perform any form of homeopathic treatment on your pet.

If you have ever seen a chiropractor or physical therapist, you have received complementary therapy, perhaps without even realizing it. Massage, focused exercise, and hydrotherapy (water) are all important components of these new-meets-old approaches. These techniques may be used to treat your Papillon if he suffers from arthritis, cruciate ligament problems, hip dysplasia, or a spinal injury.

The Tellington TTouch is a well-known form of animal massage therapy. Created by Linda Tellington-Jones in 1978, this technique uses various types of touches, lifts, and movement exercises. Now used throughout the world, it has been extremely effective in correcting behavior problems (such as aggression and chewing), improving quality of life for aging pets, and even helping with car sickness.

If you are interested in seeking this type of care for your pet, use the same amount of scrutiny in choosing a holistic caregiver as you would in selecting a veterinarian. Veterinary acupuncturists and chiropractors should be certified by the American Academy of Veterinary Acupuncture (AAVA) or the American Veterinary Chiropractic Association (ACVA). Although there is currently no certification process for canine physical therapists, the best options are those who are either licensed veterinarians themselves or willing to work in conjunction with vets.

It is also essential to understand that each dog and individual situation is different. What helps one animal may not work for another. The key is remaining open to the full range of choices available to you as a pet owner so you can find the best solution for you and your pet.

Canine Depression

Although many pet owners think that clinical depression is a condition that strikes only people, pets too can suffer from this debilitating problem. Also, as with people, dogs can suffer from depression resulting from a chemical imbalance in the brain.

If your dog seems uninterested in daily activities like eating, playing, or going for walks— and these symptoms last for more than a week—he may be depressed. Treatments for canine depression range from behavioral approaches (increased physical activity, socialization, even enrolling your pet in doggy day care) to pharmacological intervention. Prescription antidepressants, as well as natural supplements, are both commonly used to treat canine depression. Once your dog has been diagnosed, your vet can help you create the best treatment plan for him.

Also, although many of these modalities have a history of being safe and effective when properly applied, you should never perform any alternative therapy or use any form of complementary medicine without proper instruction from a qualified provider. Similarly, always remember that no procedure should ever be used as a substitute for licensed veterinary care. If you'd like to learn more about these topics, many good books and instructional videos are available at your local pet supply store or online.

EMERGENCY FIRST AID

In the face of a medical crisis, the most important thing to do is often the most difficult—remain calm. Not only can rash actions spurred by anxiety make your dog's situation worse, but animals possess an uncanny ability to sense a human's nervousness. You can unintentionally scare your Papillon if you don't pay attention to your own verbal and physical reactions.

In the event of an emergency, bring your dog to the closest veterinarian immediately, calling ahead to let the hospital know you are on your way if possible. Also, depending on the type of emergency, you may be able to do things that ensure a positive outcome, such as apply first aid. If you aren't sure what to do, get instructions from your veterinarian. Canine first aid differs dramatically from our human perceptions of emergency care because a dog's body is very different from ours in many ways. Medical doctors are taught very early in their careers that the first rule of medicine is to do no harm. This is also excellent advice for pet owners. Never give your dog any medications without first checking with your veterinarian. Drugs that can help people, such as acetaminophen and ibuprofen, can be fatal to animals. Also, procedures such as the Heimlich maneuver need to be performed very differently on a choking Papillon than on a 200-pound man. It can't be overstated that being prepared for an emergency and knowing how to appropriately handle the situation can save your dog's life.

Canine CPR

CPR stands for cardiopulmonary resuscitation, a combination of rescue breathing and chest compressions delivered to victims of cardiac arrest. Regularly used on humans, this technique

Common Dog-Related Emergencies

The following are common dog-related emergencies:

- bleeding
- fractures
- shock
- burns
- choking
- cuts and abrasions
- heatstroke
- frostbite and hypothermia
- poisoning
- snakebites
- insect bites and stings
- seizures

Emergency first-aid procedures can increase your dog's chances of a full recovery.

can also be used on animals in similar emergency situations. The worst time to learn canine CPR, however, is during an emergency. Ask your veterinarian if any organizations in your area offer courses in canine CPR. If your Papillon is not breathing, and you do not know how to perform canine CPR, bring him to a veterinarian at once.

Choking

Choking may have a number of possible causes, including any small object that can get lodged in your Papillon's trachea. Choking is a veterinary emergency, and immediate assistance is necessary. An animal who is choking may drool, gag, struggle to breathe, paw at his face, and regurgitate.

If you think your Papillon is choking, first remove his collar (if present), and then examine the inside of his mouth. It is very important that you do not simply pull on any object you may feel in your dog's throat because dogs have small bones supporting the base of their tongues that can easily be mistaken for the object in question. If you cannot identify or remove the

If your Papillon is exposed to very hot temperatures, and you see the following symptoms, it may be heatstroke:

- dazed expression
- increased heart/pulse rate
- moisture accumulating on feet
- rapid mouth breathing
- reddened gums
- thickened saliva
- vomiting

object, lift your Papillon up with his head pointing downwards, which might dislodge the object.

If these methods don't work, perform a modified Heimlich maneuver. Hold your dog around his waist so his bottom is closest to you, and place a fist just behind his ribs. Compress the abdomen several times with quick upward pressure (begin with three times), and again check his mouth. Even if you are able to dislodge the object and your dog appears fine, it is a good idea to see your veterinarian immediately in case any internal injury was incurred. This is especially important due to your Papillon's small size.

Cuts

Lacerations to paws and pads are among the most common canine injuries. If your Papillon experiences a serious cut, apply a gauze pad soaked in cold water to the wound, then contact your veterinarian. Do not use absorbent cotton because it can adhere to the cut and leave fibers in the wound. If blood is spurting from the wound, your dog has most likely severed an artery and must be taken to a veterinary hospital immediately.

Less serious wounds, on the other hand, can be treated at home. Apply firm pressure over the cut with a wet gauze pad to stop minor bleeding. Silver nitrate sticks are also useful for speeding the clotting process. To prevent debris from contaminating the wound, flush it with wound-cleaning solution, saline solution, or plain water before covering it. Once the bleeding has stopped and the laceration has been cleaned, cover the wound with a nonstick pad, and secure it with a bandage. If you are unsure about the severity of the cut, err on the side of caution and head to your vet's office.

Dehydration and Heatstroke

Dehydration and heatstroke are usually highly preventable problems. Although your Papillon may love the sun, pay attention to your local weather forecast and any warnings of especially dangerous times to be outdoors. Because dogs only have sweat glands on the pads of their feet, they cannot lose heat through sweating like humans do. Instead, they pant, which is the first sign that they need water and shelter from the heat. Remember, if you feel hot and thirsty, most likely your dog does, too. Always provide plenty of fresh drinking water for your Papillon when spending time outdoors, and keep him indoors on especially stifling days.

If you suspect that your Papillon is suffering from heatstroke, place him in a tub of cool water or gently wrap him in a towel soaked with cold water. Never use ice-cold water because this can send your dog into shock. Once your dog's temperature is lowered to 103°F (39°C), seek veterinary care at once (a rectal thermometer can provide you with an accurate reading).

Eye Injuries

Eye injuries require prompt veterinary care. Abrasions, lacerations, or punctures to the eye will cause your dog to keep his eye tightly closed, so you will unlikely be able to do much to help him yourself. If your dog has something stuck in his eye, try flushing the area with irrigation fluid or saline solution, but get him to your veterinarian to determine whether the object has scratched the cornea. If a chemical irritant was involved, flush the eye as much as possible yourself, then bring your dog to your veterinarian as

Your Papillon's First-Aid Kit

The following items should always be kept on hand in the event of a medical emergency:

- antibiotic ointment
- canine first-aid manual
- children's diphenhydramine (antihistamine)
- corn syrup
- cotton swabs
- emergency phone numbers (including poison control, emergency veterinarian, and your dog's regular vet)
- hydrogen peroxide
- instant ice pack
- ipecac syrup

- liquid bandages
- nonstick gauze pads, gauze, and tape
- oral syringe or eyedropper
- rectal thermometer
- saline solution
- scissors
- soap
- styptic powder or pencil
- tweezers
- any other item your veterinarian recommends keeping on hand

Remember to keep an eye on expiration dates and toss any out-of-date products.

quickly as possible. If both eyes seem to be affected, a chemical irritant is likely the cause of the problem.

Encounters With Other Animals

Bites from other animals require prompt veterinary attention. This is especially important for a Papillon because even a small bite from another animal can be catastrophic to this toy breed. Also, never assume that a neighborhood dog's vaccinations are current. Even if the owner assures you that they are, getting your Papillon to the vet as quickly as possible ensures the best possible outcome.

If a wild animal (such as a skunk or a raccoon) bites your dog, get him to the vet immediately. Rabies, a viral disease that can affect any warm-blooded animal, is common in many wild species. There is no treatment for rabies, but your vet may want to give your dog a rabies booster immediately following a wild-animal bite. Even if an animal doesn't look rabid, he can still suffer from this deadly disease.

If a skunk has merely sprayed your dog, check his eyes. If they are red and watery, your dog may have been hit directly in the face. Skunk spray will not cause any permanent damage, but it can be very painful and may cause temporary blindness. If your Papillon has been sprayed in the face, veterinary care should be sought. Although old-fashioned remedies such as bathing a dog in tomato juice or vinegar are still often used to treat skunk odor, they likely only mask the smell. A better option is to bathe your pet in a quart of 3-percent hydrogen peroxide mixed with ¼ cup of baking soda and a teaspoon of dishwashing liquid. Wet your dog thoroughly before applying the solution, and take care to keep it away from his eyes, nose, and mouth. The mixture will fizz. This fizz can explode if the mixture is stored in a sealed container, so discard any unused portion.

Insect Stings

Insect stings can be extremely dangerous. Bee and wasp stings in particular can cause very quick and severe reactions, but these effects are more rapid in small dogs. If your Papillon is stung, call your veterinarian at once. Ice can help reduce swelling; a swollen muzzle is often an indication of a bee sting. Keep some children's diphenhydramine (a common antihistamine used to

ASPCA Poison Control Hotline

The ASPCA Animal Poison Control Center offers an emergency hotline at 1-888-426-4435. You can call any time, 24 hours a day, 365 days a year. You will be asked the name and the amount of the toxin your dog was exposed to and the length of time that has passed; the breed, age, sex, and weight of your dog; and the symptoms he is displaying. You will also need to provide your name, address, telephone number, and credit card information (there is a small charge per case).

treat allergic reactions) on hand, and ask your vet for the correct dosage for your dog. This medicine could save your dog's life if he experiences a severe reaction to an insect sting.

Poison

When we think of poisonous substances dangerous to canines, a handful of obvious substances stand out among the rest, such as chocolate, onions, certain houseplants, and many human medications. But we must also remember that poisons don't always have to be swallowed by your dog to pose a threat. Many chemicals and toxins can be eaten, inhaled, or absorbed into the skin—sometimes even without an owner's knowledge.

When a previously healthy dog suddenly becomes ill with no apparent explanation, poisoning is frequently suspected. Signs of poisoning may include vomiting, diarrhea, and trembling, but many chemical toxins do not trigger distinctive signs of illness. This makes identification of the toxin nearly impossible in most cases. If you have reason to believe that your dog has been exposed to any kind of poison, seek advice from a qualified professional immediately. The ASPCA Animal Poison Control Center offers an emergency hotline at 1-888-426-4435, which is available 24 hours a day, 365 days a year.

Although ipecac syrup can readily induce vomiting, depending on the type of poisoning, this approach may not be prudent. Caustic toxins, such as drain cleaner, can burn the throat a second time when brought back up through the esophagus. If there is any question as to what kind of poison your dog has ingested, wait for instructions from a poison control expert before doing anything.

Trauma

If your dog experiences trauma, a severe injury, or shock to the body from a fall or other accident, get him to a veterinarian as soon as possible. Extreme care needs to be used when moving an injured animal, but to help your dog, you must first protect yourself. Injured animals can act aggressively, and they may not even recognize their beloved owners. Never get too close to an injured animal's face. Papillons may be little, but they can deliver a serious bite nonetheless, especially when in pain. Also, there may be a specific way in which you should move or

Normal Vital Signs

Illnesses and poisonings can cause a change in one or all of your dog's vital signs. Familiarize yourself with them so that you can judge the seriousness of your dog's condition should a problem arise:

- A dog's normal temperature is 99.5ºF to 102.8ºF.
- A dog's normal heart rate is 60 to 120 beats per minute.
- A dog normally takes 14 to 22 breaths per minute.

handle your dog, so whenever possible contact the veterinary hospital before doing anything.

Check for obvious injuries such as bleeding or distorted limbs. If an appendage is bleeding profusely, a rubber band can serve as a makeshift tourniquet in an emergency. If a bone appears to be fractured or broken, use care not to handle it when moving your dog. Very gently move him onto a stiff surface, if possible—a board makes a great impromptu stretcher but a blanket or a coat will suffice if nothing else is available. If you are alone and cannot hold your dog in place, use a belt or a rope to secure him for the ride to the veterinary hospital. Use rolled towels or another coat to keep him warm and prevent him from moving around. Keeping your dog as still as possible can prevent further injury from occurring on your way to the vet's office.

SENIOR CARE

As your Papillon gets older, he may experience one or more health problems common to aging pets. These can include arthritis, constipation, incontinence, vision problems, and tooth decay. The best defense against all of these issues is regular  preventive care. This not only means bringing your dog for his annual or biannual exams, but also taking steps to make his life a little more comfortable. For

Problems Common in Aging Dogs

As your Papillon ages, he may experience several different problems common in older pets. These may include arthritis, constipation, incontinence, and dental and vision problems. Although unpleasant, most age-related conditions fortunately aren't life-threatening. The key to keeping your senior feeling his best is to maintain good communication with your dog's vet, who can help ease the aches and pains many of these afflictions sometimes cause. Together, you can create a strategy for averting as many problems as possible. For example, arthritis is exacerbated by excess weight, so keeping your dog fit is fundamental. Constipation can usually be avoided with a few simple dietary changes, and you can minimize incontinence by taking your dog to his elimination spot just a bit more frequently. By brushing your dog's teeth regularly and taking him for ophthalmologic exams, you can also help prevent dental and eye diseases. You might not be able to avoid all the problems associated with aging, but you can certainly make your Papillon's golden years a lot brighter by being proactive in your approach.

Your dog's overall quality of life should be the most important factor you consider as he advances in age.

instance, when you make the transition to a senior diet, look for a variety that is available in smaller, easy-to-chew pieces, especially if your dog is missing teeth. If your dog suffers from periodontal disease, schedule a professional cleaning and have any decayed teeth removed; it will be much less painful for your pet to lose these teeth than to continue eating with them. Also, consider replacing the filling of your dog's bed or crate liner with orthopedic foam, and ask your veterinarian about adding glucosamine to your dog's diet if he suffers from arthritis.

Most importantly, keep an eye on your pet for signs of emerging or worsening problems. If your long walks are beginning to take a toll on your Papillon, it may be time to cut back to just one lap around the neighborhood, or maybe slow your pace. Getting older doesn't mean your dog will have to give up his current routine, but it may mean that changes are necessary.

Saying Goodbye

It has never seemed fair to me that the canine life span differs so dramatically from other animals. Countless other species live

Coping With the Loss of a Pet

While grief is a personal experience, you need not face loss alone. Many forms of support are available, including pet bereavement counseling services, pet-loss support hotlines, local or online internet bereavement groups, books, videos, and magazine articles. Here are a few suggestions to help you cope:

- Acknowledge your grief and give yourself permission to express it.

- Don't hesitate to reach out to others who can lend a sympathetic ear.

- Write about your feelings, either in a journal or a poem.

- Call your local humane society to see whether it offers a pet loss support group or can refer you to one. You may also want to ask your veterinarian or local animal shelter about available pet loss hotlines.

- Explore the internet for pet loss support groups and coping information.

- Prepare a memorial for your pet.

(Courtesy of the Humane Society of the United States)

decades upon decades. Chimpanzees can live well into their fifties; certain parrots can live up to twice this long; and the list goes on. If you are like me, you may wonder why there is such a drastic difference between the human life span and that of our precious dogs.

A friend once told me a story she had heard about this very subject. A child had expressed that the point of a human life was to learn to love everyone all the time and to be kind to them. Because dogs already know how to do these things, the child explained, they don't need to stay here on earth as long as we do. This conversation with my friend instantly brought a smile to my face because the theory certainly made sense.

Fortunately, due to the advancement of veterinary medicine and increasing knowledge among pet owners about the benefits of sensible nutrition, regular exercise, and other forms of preventive care, dogs are living longer than ever before. Smaller breeds, in particular, have the potential to live well into their teens. Diagnoses like cancer are no longer the inevitable death sentences they once were, and even terminal illnesses can now be treated for longer periods of time before quality of life begins to subside.

Hospice care for pets has become a notable new facet to veterinary care, making an animal's last weeks or months not only more comfortable but less stressful. More and more owners are being given this opportunity to say goodbye to their precious pets in their own homes, celebrating their animals' lives, and offering them love and dignity in their last days.

As difficult as it can be, euthanizing an animal in unmanageable pain is one of the most humane things an owner can choose to do. If you are facing this painful choice, discuss your options with your veterinarian. She can give you the clearest picture of your dog's chances for survival, and the range of effects that life-saving measures could have on him. Ultimately, you must decide if further treatment would be provided to prolong your dog's life or to postpone your own pain in letting him go. This is unquestionably the hardest choice you will ever make for your beloved pet.

If you have recently made this most excruciating decision, give yourself permission to grieve what is a very real loss. The death of a pet can be devastating. Reaching out to others can be one of the best ways to help ease your pain. Ask your veterinarian to recommend a support group for grieving pet owners, or look for one online or in your local newspaper. Sometimes just being able to talk about the loss of your dog can help.

There is no single protocol for saying goodbye to one pet and welcoming a new one into your home. Perhaps you need a few months—or even longer—before you feel ready to embark upon pet ownership once again. If so, allow yourself this important time. Conversely, you may feel that the best way to deal with your feelings of loss is by having a new pet to love and care for. Hugs and kisses can indeed be very healing, but you must be ready to provide this animal with a permanent home. If a new Papillon is in your immediate plans, take your time in selecting just the right dog for you. He's out there waiting for you to find him.

ASSOCIATIONS AND ORGANIZATIONS

Papillon Club of America
3609 Robb Ave.
Cincinnati, OH 45211-4509
www.papillonclub.org

Papillon Canada
www. papilloncanada.org

Papillon (Butterfly Dog) Club
United Kingdom
www.papillonclub.co.uk

Breed Clubs
American Kennel Club (AKC)
5580 Centerview Drive
Raleigh, NC 27606
Telephone: (919) 233-9767
Fax: (919) 233-3627
E-mail: info@akc.org
www.akc.org

Canadian Kennel Club (CKC)
89 Skyway Avenue, Suite 100
Etobicoke, Ontario M9W 6R4
Canada
Telephone: (416) 675-5511
Fax: (416) 675-6506
E-mail: information@ckc.ca
www.ckc.ca

Federation Cynologique Internationale (FCI)
Secretariat General de la FCI
Place Albert 1er, 13
B – 6530 Thuin
Belqique
www.fci.be

The Kennel Club
1 Clarges Street
London
W1J 8AB
England
Telephone: 0870 606 6750
Fax: 0207 518 1058
www.the-kennel-club.org.uk

United Kennel Club (UKC)
100 E. Kilgore Road
Kalamazoo, MI 49002-5584
Telephone: (269) 343-9020
Fax: (269) 343-7037
E-mail: pbickell@ukcdogs.com
www.ukcdogs.com

Pet Sitters
National Association of Professional Pet Sitters
15000 Commerce Parkway, Suite C
Mt. Laurel, NJ 08054
Telephone: (856) 439-0324
Fax: (856) 439-0525
E-mail: napps@ahint.com
www.petsitters.org

Pet Sitters International
201 East King Street
King, NC 27021-9161
Telephone: (336) 983-9222
Fax: (336) 983-5266
E-mail: info@petsit.com
www.petsit.com

Rescue Organizations and Animal Welfare Groups
American Humane Association (AHA)
63 Inverness Drive East
Englewood, CO 80112
Telephone: (303) 792-9900
Fax: 792-5333
www.americanhumane.org

American Society for the Prevention of Cruelty to Animals (ASPCA)
424 E. 92nd Street
New York, NY 10128-6804
Telephone: (212) 876-7700
www.aspca.org

Royal Society for the Prevention of Cruelty to Animals (RSPCA)
Telephone: 0870 3335 999
Fax: 0870 7530 284
www.rspca.org.uk

The Humane Society of the United States (HSUS)
2100 L Street, NW
Washington, DC 20037
Telephone: (202) 452-1100
www.hsus.org

Sports
Canine Freestyle Federation, Inc.
E-mail: secretary@canine-freestyle.org
www.canine-freestyle.org

International Agility Link (IAL)
Global Administrator: Steve Drinkwater
E-mail: yunde@powerup.au
www.agilityclick.com/~ial

North American Dog Agility Council
11522 South Hwy 3
Cataldo, ID 83810
www.nadac.com

North American Flyball Association
www.flyball.org
1400 West Devon Avenue #512
Chicago, IL 60660
800-318-6312

United States Dog Agility Association
P.O. Box 850955
Richardson, TX 75085-0955
Telephone: (972) 487-2200
www.usdaa.com

World Canine Freestyle Organization
P.O. Box 350122
Brooklyn, NY 11235-2525
Telephone: (718) 332-8336
www.worldcaninefreestyle.org

Therapy
Delta Society
875 124th Ave NE, Suite 101
Bellevue, WA 98005
Telephone: (425) 226-7357
Fax: (425) 235-1076
E-mail: info@deltasociety.org
www.deltasociety.org

Therapy Dogs Incorporated
P.O. Box 5868
Cheyenne, WY 82003
Telephone: (877) 843-7364
E-mail: therdog@sisna.com
www.therapydogs.com

Therapy Dogs International (TDI)
88 Bartley Road
Flanders, NJ 07836
Telephone: (973) 252-9800
Fax: (973) 252-7171
E-mail: tdi@gti.net
www.tdi-dog.org

Training
Animal Behavior Society
www.animalbehavior.org

Association of Pet Dog Trainers (APDT)
150 Executive Center Drive
Box 35
Greenville, SC 29615
Telephone: (800) PET-DOGS
Fax: (864) 331-0767
E-mail: information@apdt.com
www.apdt.com

National Association of Dog Obedience Instructors (NADOI)
PMB 369
729 Grapevine Hwy.
Hurst, TX 76054-2085
www.nadoi.org

Veterinary and Health Resources
Academy of Veterinary Homeopathy (AVH)
P.O. Box 9280
Wilmington, DE 19809
Telephone: (866) 652-1590
Fax: (866) 652-1590
E-mail: office@TheAVH.org
www.theavh.org

American Academy of Veterinary Acupuncture (AAVA)
100 Roscommon Drive, Suite 320
Middletown, CT 06457
Telephone: (860) 635-6300
Fax: (860) 635-6400
E-mail: office@aava.org
www.aava.org

American Animal Hospital Association (AAHA)
P.O. Box 150899
Denver, CO 80215-0899
Telephone: (303) 986-2800
Fax: (303) 986-1700
E-mail: info@aahanet.org
www.aahanet.org/index.cfm

**American College of
Veterinary Internal
Medicine (ACVIM)**
1997 Wadsworth Blvd.,
Suite A
Lakewood, CO 80214-5293
Telephone: (800) 245-9081
Fax: (303) 231-0880
E-mail: ACVIM@ACVIM.org
www.acvim.org

**American College
of Veterinary
Ophthalmologists (ACVO)**
P.O. Box 1311
Meridian, ID 83860
Telephone: (208) 466-7624
Fax: (208) 466-7693
E-mail: office@acvo.com
www.acvo.com

**American Holistic
Veterinary Medical
Association (AHVMA)**
2218 Old Emmorton Road
Bel Air, MD 21015
Telephone: (410) 569-0795
Fax: (410) 569-2346
E-mail: office@ahvma.org
www.ahvma.org

**American Veterinary
Medical Association
(AVMA)**
1931 North Meacham Road,
Suite 100
Schaumburg, IL 60173
Telephone: (847) 925-8070
Fax: (847) 925-1329
E-mail: avmainfo@avma.org
www.avma.org

**ASPCA Animal Poison
Control Center**
1717 South Philo Road,
Suite 36
Urbana, IL 61802
Telephone: (888) 426-4435
www.aspca.org

**British Veterinary
Association (BVA)**
7 Mansfield Street
London
W1G 9NQ
England
Telephone: 020 7636 6541
Fax: 020 7436 2970
E-mail: bvahq@bva.co.uk
www.bva.co.uk

**Canine Eye Registration
Foundation (CERF)**
VMDB/CERF
1248 Lynn Hall
625 Harrison St.
Purdue University
West Lafayette, IN
47907-2026
Telephone: (765) 494-8179
E-mail: CERF@vmbd.org
www.vmdb.org

**Orthopedic Foundation for
Animals (OFA)**
2300 N.E. Nifong Blvd.
Columbus, MI
65201-3856
Telephone: (573) 442-0418
Fax: (573) 875-5073
E-mail: ofa@offa.org
www.offa.org

PUBLICATIONS

Books
Goldstein, Robert S., V.M.D.,
and Susan J. *The Goldsteins'
Wellness & Longevity
Program*. Neptune City:
T.F.H. Publications, 2005.

Morgan, Diane. *Good
Dogkeeping*. Neptune City:
T.F.H. Publications, 2005

Magazines
AKC *Family Dog*
American Kennel Club
260 Madison Avenue
New York, NY 10016
Telephone: (800) 490-5675
E-mail: familydog@akc.org
www.akc.org/pubs/
familydog

AKC *Gazette*
American Kennel Club
260 Madison Avenue
New York, NY 10016
Telephone: (800) 533-7323
E-mail: gazette@akc.org
www.akc.org/pubs/gazette

Dog & Kennel
Pet Publishing, Inc.
7-L Dundas Circle
Greensboro, NC 27407
Telephone: (336) 292-4272
Fax: (336) 292-4272
E-mail: info@petpublishing.
com
www.dogandkennel.com

Dog Fancy
Subscription Department
P.O. Box 53264
Boulder, CO 80322-3264
Telephone: (800) 365-4421
E-mail: barkback@dogfancy.
com
www.dogfancy.com

Dogs Monthly
Ascot House
High Street, Ascot,
Berkshire SL5 7JG
United Kingdom
Telephone: 0870 730 8433
Fax: 0870 730 8431
E-mail: admin@rtc-
associates.freeserve.co.uk
www.corsini.co.uk/
dogsmonthly

Note: **Boldfaced** numbers indicate illustrations.

DEDICATION

To Barbara Dalvet—for *Sunflowers*, *Borrowers*, and endless possibilities...

ABOUT THE AUTHOR

Tammy Gagne is a freelance writer who specializes in the health and behavior of companion animals. In addition to being a regular contributor to several national pet care magazines, she has authored numerous books for both adults and children. Other dog-related titles include *Bulldogs, The Cocker Spaniel, The Chihuahua, The English Springer Spaniel*, and *The Happy Adopted Dog*. An avid dog lover, Tammy has owned purebred dogs for more than 25 years. She resides in northern New England with her husband, son, dogs, and parrots.

PHOTO CREDITS

Paul Cotney (Shutterstock): 70, 95, 127, 172, 177, 181
Waldemar Dabrowski (Shutterstock): 14, 58
Ilya D. Gridnev (Shutterstock): 193
Cindy Hughes (Shutterstock): 113
Dee Hunter (Shutterstock): 51
Eric Isselée (Shutterstock): 11, 107, 132
Marcel Jancovic (Shutterstock): 19, 21, 28, 45, 47, 80, 108, 118, 124, 168, 176
Donald Joski (Shutterstock): 166
Jay Kim (Shutterstock): 26
Sergey Lavrentev (Shutterstock): 17, 41, 53, 72, 74, 76, 79, 83, 90, 111, 121, 134, 138, 154, 156, 159, 195, 196, 198, 200, 202, 204
Suponev Vladimir Mihajlovich (Shutterstock): 10, 153
Tootles (Shutterstock): 48
HTuller (Shutterstock): 44, 60
April Turner (Shutterstock): 59
Diane Webb (Shutterstock): 23

Sidebars (Shutterstock): Paul Cotney, Sergey Lavrentev, Suponev Vladimir Mihajlovich
All other photos courtesy of Isabelle Francais, Shutterstock, and TFH Archives

Front cover: Paul Cotney
Back cover: Sergey Lavrentev

NATURAL with added VITAMINS

Nutri Dent®

Promotes Optimal Dental Health!

Visit
nylabone.com
Join Club NYLA!
get coupons &
product
information

360° Design
Cleaning Action!™

USA MADE

Dog's L♥ve 'em!™

AVAILABLE IN MULTIPLE SIZES AND FLAVORS.

Nylabone®

Trusted for Over 50 Years

Our Mission with Nutri Dent® is to promote optimal dental health for dogs
through a trusted, natural, delicious chew that provides effective cleaning action...
GUARANTEED to make your dog go wild with anticipation and happiness!!!

Nylabone Products • P.O. Box 427, Neptune, NJ 07754-0427 • 1-800-631-2188 • Fax: 732-988-5466
www.nylabone.com • info@nylabone.com • For more information contact your sales representative or contact us at sales@tfh.com